D0721403

BB

armoured onslaught:
8th August 1918

Douglas Orgill

Editor-in-Chief: Barrie Pitt
Editor: David Mason
Art Director: Sarah Kingham
Picture Editor: Robert Hunt
Consultant Art Editor: Denis Piper
Designer: David A Evans
Illustration: John Batchelor
Photographic Research: Jonathan Moore
Cartographer: Richard Natkiel

Contents

'Secure and covered chariots'

Introduction by Peter Elstob

In August 1944, exactly twenty-six years after the first tanks breached the hitherto impregnable German defences, British tanks were again in full pursuit of a shattered German army retreating across the old battle-fields. As the village names – Bapaume, Bayonvillers, Cerisy and Morcourt appeared on our 'Charlie Love' – as the centre line of the advance was called in the innocent belief that it foxed German Intelligence – we remembered those lectures delivered in fuggy Nissen huts on the history of the Royal Tank Regiment. Wasn't this the village from which a German field battery had knocked out seven of our tanks in quick succession? And wasn't it here in the lovely Somme Valley that eleven of the new Mark V stars had been destroyed? Although we ourselves had met very little opposition in the 125-mile advance from the Seine during the last three days, experience had taught us to respect our opposite numbers in the Panzer Corps, and to know that another clash with them undoubtedly awaited us somewhere. Perhaps history would repeat itself and we should fight once again in that part of France where tanks had 'come of age'.

But, of course, in the evolution of war, history rarely repeats itself, and by 1944 it was accepted that although tanks may be delayed by anti-tank weapons, because of their precious mobility they can only be defeated by other tanks. And so we swept on, past the scenes of the historical armoured breakthrough so well described by Douglas Orgill in this book, to meet the German armour on the field of their choice, the flat, canal-scarred land of Holland.

The hot house of war increases the numbers of weapons and forces their evolution; the cold that follows checks both drastically as defence budgets are slashed and plans of the greatest boldness grow yellow in the files. When the first, clumsy British tanks lumbered through the German wire and blasted away the machine-gun positions in 1916, both sides were surprised, but the real surprise is that it took so long after the invention of the internal combustion engine to realise so old an idea. Leonardo da Vinci had noted in 1482, 'I am building secure and covered chariots and when they advance with their guns into the midst of the foe even the largest of enemy masses must retreat and behind them the infantry can follow in safety and without opposition'.

This same concept came up time and again in the succeeding centuries only to be dismissed as impossible because the power necessary to manoeuvre such unwieldy masses did not exist. But by 1914 it did, and workable plans for a mobile fort or 'landship' were ready within ten weeks of the outbreak of war. Yet it was not until the Somme offensive in September 1916 that forty-nine Mark Is were ready for their trial by battle, and even that small number would not have been possible had it not been for the dedication of a few stubborn men who persevered in the face of that opposition to anything new which is one of the less admirable traditions of the British Army.

The inevitable shortcomings of green crews and untried tanks were

made much of by those who had opposed the new arm from its beginnings, but the wire *had* been breached, the mighty machine-gun had been toppled and the terror of the enemy had been real enough. It was evident to all fair-minded men that here was a new, perhaps even a decisive, weapon. Haig was one of these and only four days after the tanks' baptism he sent DCGS to the War Office with a request for one thousand tanks, heavier than Mark Is and with improved armour.

The result was an order for another hundred Mark Is. But the battle tank evolved despite powerful opposition and discouraging setbacks, from a simple mobile machine-gun destroyer to the decisive tactical weapon by which, at last, the great German defences were broken.

The tanks finally had their day – a day which was to change the face of warfare completely – and in *Armoured Onslaught* the story is told with a completeness and clarity which is unmatched.

Immediately far-reaching plans for the use of armour in 1919 were laid. The Americans were to build 6,000 Allied Tanks, an improved version of the Mark V double star which mounted a machine-gun and a 6-pounder on each side; the British ordered 3,000 tanks to be built, including 1,000 of the new, fast, manoeuvrable Medium Ds and it was planned to land a mixed tank/infantry force on the Belgian coast at the same time as a great assault, on the lines of Fuller's famous 'Plan 1919', was mounted. In this attack nearly 5,000 tanks in three waves were to be launched: a 'Disorganising Force' to overrun the German headquarters, a 'Breaking Force' of 54 battalions of heavy tanks and a 'Pursuing Force' to maintain the disarray.

But with the Armistice the flow of money dried up and in the years that followed tank men in Britain and America had to fight to keep their arm in existence while in Germany new soldiers quietly analysed the use of tanks in the last war and the far-seeing writings of Fuller and Liddell Hart were made required reading for tank officers. The Blitzkrieg that stunned Europe in the summer of 1940 was a logical extension of the brilliant tactics of the armoured breakthrough at Amiens twenty-one years earlier.

The deadlock

7259

Gustav Liersch & Co.

It might be said in retrospect that the first half of the First World War was spent in the search for a weapon. Yet it had been clear for several decades that though the principles of war remained the same, its whole nature and technique were changing. The Franco-Prussian War of 1870, and later the struggle between the British and the Boers in South Africa, had revealed that the battlefields of the future would be quite unlike those of the past, and that a great war between major contestants would inevitably pose military problems to which there was, as yet, no military solution.

These problems revolved around the combination of manoeuvre and fire-power. For centuries, manoeuvre had been the province of the cavalry, but by 1914, although the military establishments of Britain and Europe firmly refused to recognise the fact, the cavalry was out of date. By the end of 1914, a man could have walked by trench from Switzerland to the Channel, and the battlefield on either side of the front line was ruled by a deadly trinity – the machine gun, the quick-firing field gun, and the seemingly endless miles of rusting barbed wire. Cavalry action under such conditions was shown again and again to be hopeless, yet it seemed that without cavalry, manoeuvre could not be re-established on the battlefield. Manoeuvre was essential for proper generalship, and proper generalship, in turn, was the only way to avoid the shocking casualties which had already destroyed half a generation of young men. Generals could no longer march and wheel and strike at flanks. There were no flanks. There was only the wire-strewn, trench-seamed, machine-gun-guarded line. Repeated attempts by both sides to break this by driving in enormous salients invariably failed under the weight of firepower which the defences were able to bring to bear. A policy of attrition, with the

numbing casualties which such a policy demanded, was reluctantly accepted by each side as the means of defeating the other.

Up to 1916, only two techniques were put forward in an attempt to break the military deadlock. The first was artillery – the attempt by concentrated bombardment to destroy trench systems in depth so that, in theory at any rate, the cavalry could have its ride to glory. Alas, as the smoke cleared after each bigger and better bombardment, the machine guns still waited in the angles of ruined trenches to meet the attacking men and horses as they scrambled forward over the shattered coils of wire.

The second bid to solve the problem was gas, used by the Germans at the Second Battles of Ypres in the spring of 1915. This, too, proved impracticable as a decisive weapon – partly because of the westerly nature of the prevailing winds in the area, partly because the Allies reacted quickly by the provision of simple respirators for their troops. Gas soon became, like the machine gun and the field gun, one more useful but indecisive part of the armoury of each side. By the end of 1915 the absence from the battlefield of two of the most important principles of war – surprise and mobility – was still lengthening the casualty lists in the newspapers of London, Paris and Berlin. The war was a siege war, with all the blood and misery which that entailed.

The answer to siege war, when eventually it came, was based, inevitably, upon the device which was to change the face of the future – the internal combustion engine. Even at the beginning of the war, however, the internal combustion engine was not wholly a stranger to the battlefield. Armoured cars had made their appearance in 1914, under the auspices of the British Admiralty Air Division, and the idea was taken further in the same year by Colonel Ernest Swinton, who put forward a scheme for propelling a fighting vehicle on caterpillar

A German Maxim machine gun, the new dominating factor in trench warfare

Above: 2nd Cavalry Division HQ on the Marne, September 1914. At this early stage in the war it was still expected that it would be the cavalry which would exploit any breakthrough. *Below:* Lanchester armoured car of the Royal Naval Air Service 1915. *Right:* Flanders 1915. The Germans experiment with oxygen equipment to combat a new menace in the trenches – gas

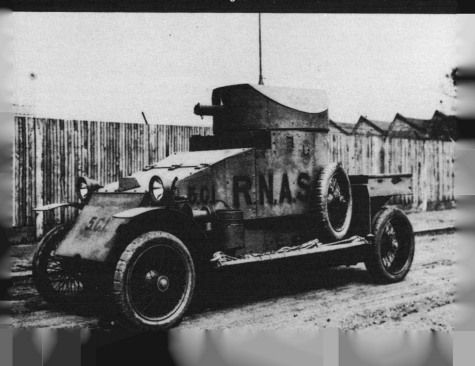

'Mother' was the name given to the world's first true tank, which later went into production as the Mark I. The tank first ran in December 1915, but official trials with the completed vehicle were not begun till early the next year. The main difference between this tank and earlier prototypes was its reversion to the 'big wheel' idea. As the big wheel had been seen to be impractical in its true form, Mother had the wheel stretched into a lozenge form, which gave good performance, but also enabled the tank to be steered adequately and to be given a relatively low profile. As with the earlier 'Little Willie', the idea of a traversing turret was considered but abandoned, as it would have made the centre of

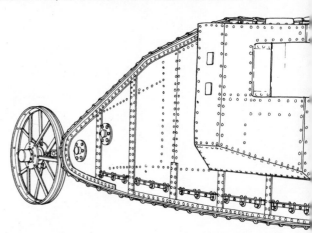

tracks. From these ideas, the tank was born.

The design and development of the prototypes of the early tanks are not the province of this account, though some description of the various battle versions is necessary if the tank battles of 1918 are to be understood.

From the first, the primary object of the tank was to help infantry forward. In order to do this it had to be capable of crushing and mangling the German defensive wire. In turn, the machine itself had to be proof against concentrated rifle and machine gun fire, though it was not envisaged, at this early stage, that it would be able to stand up to direct hits from shells. Its object, in fact, was attack: it was uncompromisingly offensive.

By 1916, engineers had produced a machine which went a long way towards meeting these demands. This was the Mark I tank, a lozenge-shaped, rhomboidal vehicle, weighing 28 tons, 8 feet high and 27 feet long, with a maximum road speed of a little over 3mph. It was formidably armed, in two versions: a male version mounting two quick-firing Hotchkiss six-pounder guns and four machine guns, and a female version with six machine guns. Each version towed a 'tail' of two large wheels which were intended to help the steering of the monster. The Mark I had a crew of eight: a commander, a driver, two gearsmen and four gunners. These men fought and worked in a fume-laden hull in which it was not possible to stand fully upright, and where the temperature in action rose to more than 100 degrees Fahrenheit. Whatever its virtues as a military innovation, the Mark I placed a very great strain on its crew.

The introduction of the Mark I to battle aroused mixed emotions in the British army. From the traditionalists, many of whom, of course, were in high commands, it brought reactions

Debut of the tank: a Mark I in Chimpanzee Valley, 15th September 1916

gravity too high. As no suitable gun was forthcoming from the army, Mother was fitted with two naval 6-pounder guns. *Weight:* **28 tons.** *Crew:* **8.** *Armament:* Two long-barrelled naval 6-pounder guns and provision for three 8-mm Hotchkiss machine guns. *Armour:* None as such, but the construction was in boiler plate, which was replaced by armour in the Mark I. *Power:* Daimler water-cooled inline, 105hp. *Speed:* **3.7 mph maximum.** *Trench crossing:* **9 feet.** *Step:* **4 feet 6 inches.** *Range:* **50 miles maximum.** *Length:* **26 feet 5 inches.** *Height:* **8 feet 2 inches.** *Width:* **13 feet 9½ inches.**

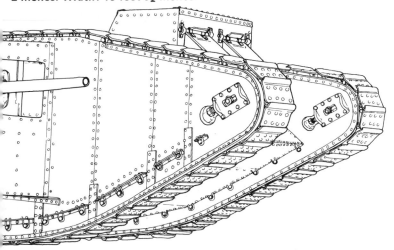

Mark I Mother tank

A knocked-out Mark I, casualty of the first day that tanks went into action, Flers-Courcelette, September 1915

ranging from doubt to derision; but there were others with clearer heads. A middle-aged British major, J F C Fuller, meeting his first tank near Crécy in August 1916, wrote afterwards:

'Here was the unknown X in the equation of victory. All that was necessary now was to get people to see the problem . . .'

This was the beginning of a long, historic, and fruitful association between Fuller and the tank, as we shall see, but getting people 'to see the problem' proved to be more difficult than he imagined.

The first tank action in history was fought by fewer than fifty Mark Is, on 15th September 1916. It was a mixed success – the tanks caused surprise and even terror wherever they appeared, but they achieved only about a

Colonel JFC Fuller. When he met his first tank in August 1916 he was convinced that 'here was the unknown X in the equation of victory'

mile of penetration round the villages of Flers-Courcelette, and many broke down or were ditched.

To many minds, in fact, the tanks' performance in battle had been unconvincing, and the more conservative elements of the British army – notably the Chief of Staff, Sir Lancelot Kiggell – were eager to relegate them to a purely accessory role, in which they would fit in with 'traditional' tactics, rather than that tactics should be radically changed to take account of the new armoured potential.

Over the next year, 1917, tanks were used – usually only in handfuls – with varying success. Where they proved of decisive value, the work was done by one or two tanks clearing a length of troublesome enemy trench: never were the machines used *en masse* as a pivotal weapon. The depths of tank

19

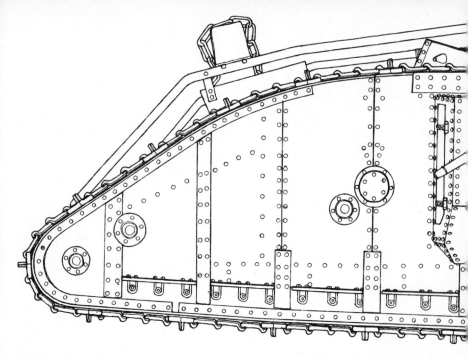

The British Mark IV was the next major model to appear after the Mark I, and incorporated the lessons learned in service with the latter. These resulted in an increase in armour thickness to combat the early German anti-tank bullets, and retractable sponsons to facilitate movement in areas behind the lines and on railways. Another improvement over the earlier model was the provision of shorter barrelled guns, as the 40-calibre guns of the Marks I, II and III had tended to bury their muzzles in the ground when the tank came down a steep descent.

Mark IVs at Cambrai, 1917

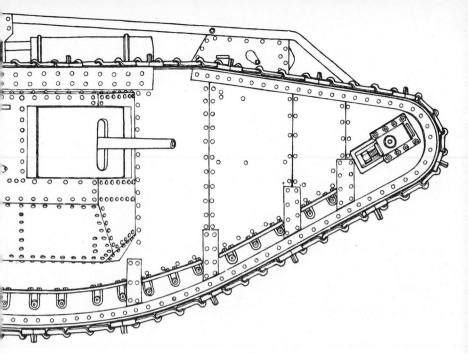

Male tanks were armed with two guns of the later 23-calibre length and four Lewis guns, while Female tanks, which were built in the ratio of 3:2 with Male tanks, were armed with six Lewis or Hotchkiss guns. 1,015 were built in all. Illustrated is a Mark IV Male. *Weight:* **28 tons (Female 26 tons).** *Crew:* **8.** *Armament:* Two 6-pounder guns with 332 rounds and four .303-inch Lewis guns with 6,272 rounds (Male); six Lewis or Hotchkiss machine guns with 30,080 rounds (Female). *Armour:* **6mm minimum and 12mm maximum.** *Power:* **Daimler water-cooled inline, 105hp.** *Speed:* **3.7 mph maximum.** *Trench crossing:* **10 feet.** *Step:* **4 feet 6 inches.** *Radius of action:* **35 miles.** *Length:* **26 feet 5 inches.** *Height:* **8 feet 2 inches.** *Width:* **12 feet 10 inches (10 feet 6 inches Female)**

Above: Direct artillery hit, Zonnebeke, September 1917. *Below:* Mark IV female with flamethrower. *Right:* His Majesty King George V inspects the Tank Corps, August 1918, accompanied by its commander, General Elles

warfare, morally and physically, were reached in the muddy swamps round Achicourt in the spring, and in the dreadful slough of Passchendaele in the autumn, when the monsters wallowed helplessly, trapped up to their sponsons in glutinous mud. It was a dispiriting time for the tank enthusiasts of the British army.

For there were such enthusiasts, and they were working hard behind the year's backcloth of frustration and despair. First of all, even the limited battle experience available had convinced the designers of the Mark I that considerable improvements must be made. The ponderous towed wheels were now removed, since it was discovered that they gave little assistance to the steering, and were themselves highly likely to be damaged by enemy shellfire. The sponsons were made smaller, and were designed so that they could be swung inboard, making it much easier for them to be moved up to the front on French railway trucks. Petrol, previously carried inside the driver's cab, was now stored in an armoured 60-gallon tank outside the hull, while the early glass prisms intended for crew observation, which had splintered dangerously under rifle and machine gun fire, were replaced by pinhole metal apertures. The machine which emerged after all these improvements was the Mark IV.

In a human sense, too, the Tank Corps – as the tank arm was finally named in June 1917 – made considerable progress. In the sphere of command, it acquired a leader and a planner. The leader was Brigadier General Hugh Elles. a traditional soldier in some respects, but a man of dash and *élan* – qualities which the Tank Corps needed during its months of trial. The planner was the Major Fuller who had, a year earlier, discerned 'the unknown X in the equation of victory'. During 1917 he became GSO 1 to Elles, and bent his questing and original mind to the problems of armoured warfare. For this task, Fuller was supremely well fitted. It was he who now

Mark IVs returning from Cambrai, with sponsons swung inboard for transport on railway trucks

urged the Tank Corps towards its first battle triumph – although, in a wider military sense, the triumph was followed by disaster.

The Battle of Cambrai which opened on 20th November 1917 was marked by the first mass use of tanks in war – 476 of them, in fact, led by Elles himself. There was no preliminary artillery barrage, and the tanks achieved al-almost complete surprise. Six miles were gained in four hours, 100 guns and 4,000 Germans captured, while in London the church bells pealed for victory. Soon, however, there was a bitter awakening. The battle, which had originally been projected by Fuller as essentially a tank raid into the Hindenburg Line, had been unsuitably expanded by the higher command into the seizing of a salient. This salient proved vulnerable to German counterattack, and soon all that had been gained was lost again, while the Germans actually improved their position by occupying part of the British line.

However, in another sense, Cambrai was of decisive importance. First, the initial success convinced some of the more intelligent doubters that tanks could achieve decisive results if they were used properly. Second, the Germans themselves drew the opposite, and wrong, conclusion. They were satisfied that they had the measure of the new machines, and that the tanks could achieve little, if resolutely opposed. As 1918 dawned it was becoming clear that the great test for both sides still lay ahead, and that, on the Allied side at least, the tank was going to play a major part. The French had already taken up the idea, and were producing several types of machine, perhaps the most effective of which was the Renault FT. This was a small, relatively fast (5mph) model, with an all-round turret traverse. There were various versions, armed with a 37mm or 75mm gun, or a heavy machine gun.

Tank and infantry casualties at Cambrai, 1917, the battle which involved the first major use of tanks in war

The Aisne, May 1918. German troops wait to advance during Ludendorff's last bid for victory

The spring and early summer of 1918 saw the launching and eventual frustration of the great German attack which was Ludendorff's last real bid to win the war. The German armies surged forward over the old Somme battlefield, and by May had reached to within forty miles of Paris. But the Allied line still held, and behind it the armies of Foch and Haig were being swollen by the arrival of nearly thirty American divisions. As spring grew into summer, the German armies had reached an *impasse*, caught in a salient which had been achieved at a cost of much blood and suffering, and which could yet turn out to be a trap.

Tank Mark IV. *Weight:* 28 tons. *Length:* 26 feet 5 inches. *Height:* 8 feet 2 inches. *Width (over sponsons):* 12 feet 10 inches. *Power:* Daimler 6-cylinder inline, water-cooled, 105hp at 1,000rpm. *Speed:* 3.7mph maximum. *Step:* 4 feet 6 inches. *Trench:* 10 feet. *Range:* 70 miles. *Armament:* Two Hotchkiss 23-calibre 6-pounder guns with 204 rounds and three .303-inch Lewis guns wth 5,640 rounds. *Armour:* 16mm front, 12mm sides and rear, 8mm roof and belly. *Crew:* 8 (driver, commander, two 6-pounder gunners, two machine gunners and two brakemen)

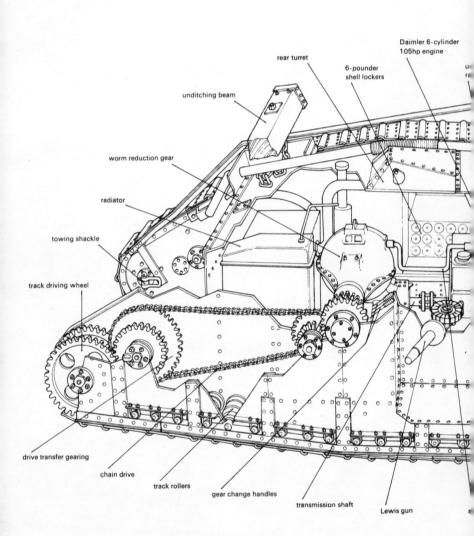

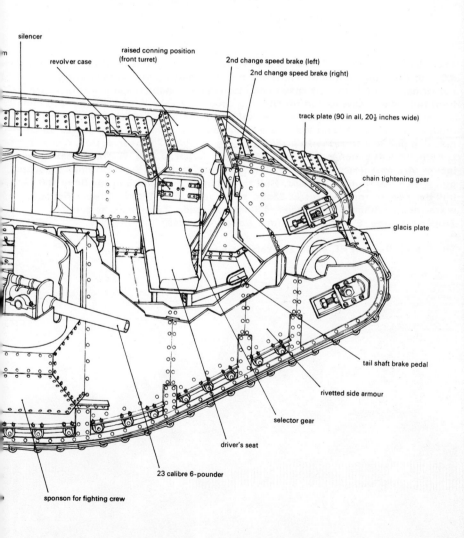

silencer

m

revolver case

raised conning position
(front turret)

2nd change speed brake (left)

2nd change speed brake (right)

track plate (90 in all, 20½ inches wide)

chain tightening gear

glacis plate

tail shaft brake pedal

rivetted side armour

selector gear

driver's seat

23 calibre 6-pounder

sponson for fighting crew

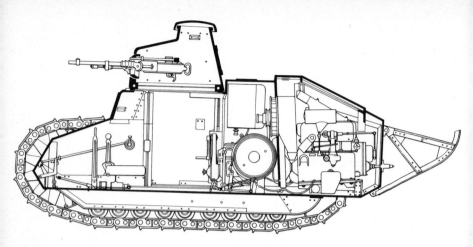

The French Renault FT17 was the best light tank of the First World War, and about 4,000 of the type were built. Light and handy, it had a good cross country performance, a fair turn of speed and reasonable trench crossing abilities with its light tailpiece. It saw action for the first time in May 1918, and was used by the armies of France, the United States, Italian and Belgian armies. The two main models of the First World War were equipped with either a 37mm gun or an 8mm machine gun in a turret with a 360° traverse. *Weight:* 7 tons in action. *Crew:* 2. *Length:* 16 feet 5 inches (with the tailpiece). *Height:* 7 feet. *Width:* 5 feet 7½ inches. *Armament:* One 37mm gun with 237 rounds or one 8mm Hotchkiss machine gun with 4,800 rounds. *Armour:* Hull front 16mm, hullsides and top 8mm and hull belly 6mm; rounded turret 22mm, octagonal turret 16mm. *Power:* Renault water-cooled inline, 35hp. *Speed:* 4.8 mph on roads, 2.2 mph cross country. *Trench crossing:* 6 feet. *Step:* 2 feet. *Range:* 22 miles

The French Renault FT, small and relatively fast

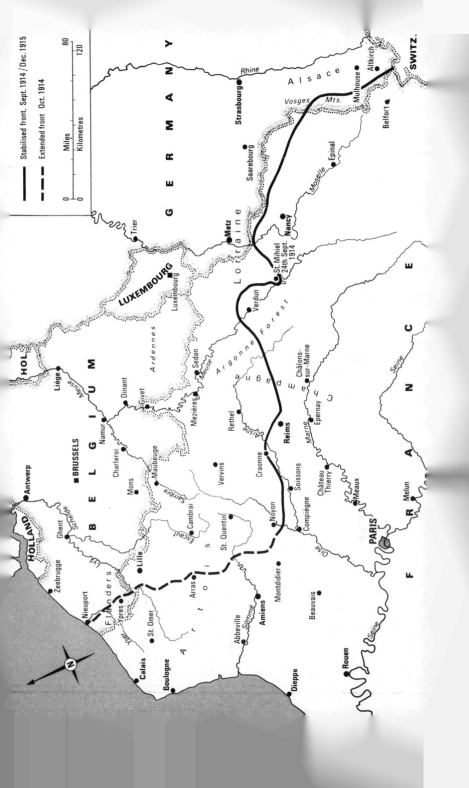

The Monash method

As June opened, the position of the opposing armies could be summarised by saying that the German offensive had failed north of the Somme and in front of Amiens; that it had failed, after big initial advances, on the River Lys; and that after the wearing struggle with the French on the Chemin des Dames – a long ridge lying between the Rivers Aisne and Ailette – it had lapped down as far as the Marne and then finally stopped.

South of the Somme, the British front was at last relatively quiet. The British command was now casting about for some limited form of offensive action. The Commander-in-Chief, Sir Douglas Haig, had three things in mind. First, he wished to improve morale by demonstrating once more that the Germans did not hold all the initiative. Second, he wished to find out how German morale had reacted to the inevitable disappointment of the failure to achieve a decisive advance in the spring offensive. Third, he wished to secure better jumping-off points for a potential offensive later in the year.

The instrument for his purpose was the Fourth Army, which consisted of the Australian Corps and the British III Corps. Thus the intended operation would depend upon the cooperation of two of the most remarkable soldiers on the Allied side – the army commander himself, General Sir Henry Rawlinson, and the Australian corps commander, Lieutenant-General John Monash. These two men were among the chief *dramatis personae* of the events that were now to follow, and yet both of them – Rawlinson, especially, perhaps – have been almost forgotten.

Rawlinson was fifty-four years old, a baronet who had fought at Omdurman in 1898, and had been at Ladysmith in the struggle with the Boers. He was a man of restless and inquiring mind but, like others, he had found little scope for his imagination in the rigid realities of the Western Front. His experiences so far had been chas-

tening, and would perhaps have destroyed a lesser man. He had played a key part in the dreadful battle of the Somme – and those were weeks which left their mark on every man, high or low, in the British armies which took part. What saved Rawlinson was his temperament, and his willingness to discard academic theory and allow himself to be guided by experience. He had, wrote a military colleague, 'humour, tact, and kindliness, and responsive comprehension of the difficulties of others . . .' These gentlemanly qualities of Rawlinson, formidably allied to a shrewd, driving intelligence, were to be vital to him in the weeks ahead in his successful relationship with his rather prickly and independent corps commander, Monash.

Monash was one of the most unusual of the senior commanders on either side. His background alone was unique for an officer of high rank. His parents were German Jews who had emigrated to Australia, and he himself was not a career soldier like those around him, but a civil engineer who had reached his rank after enrolment in Australia's Citizen Forces in 1913 – and, incidentally, a spell as chief censor for Australia after war broke out. Moreover, he was not – in the conventional sense – a front-line soldier with a boyish disdain for risks, which was an attractive though vulnerable part of the temperaments of British and German officers of a more traditional mould.

To Monash, battle was an engineering problem. He was a cost-analysis soldier, and – like Montgomery a generation later – was determined to fight no battle unless he was sure previously that he would win it. This man was now to use tanks in the most advanced and successful way that had yet been achieved – and yet, paradoxically, he was at heart an infantryman who saw the role of the infantry as paramount in war. In later years he summed it up with clarity:

'I had formed the theory that the true role of the infantry was not to

Above: The Germans push on over the Ailette Canal. *Below left:* Field-Marshal Sir Douglas Haig, the British Commander-in-Chief. *Below right:* General Sir Henry Rawlinson, commander of British Fourth Army

expend itself upon heroic physical effort, nor to wither away under merciless machine gun fire, nor to impale itself on hostile bayonets, nor to tear itself to pieces in hostile entanglements: but, on the contrary, to advance under the maximum possible array of mechanical resources, in the form of guns, machine guns, tanks, mortars and aeroplanes: to advance with as little impediment as possible: to be relieved as far as possible of the obligation to fight their way forward: to march, resolutely, regardless of the din and tumult of battle, to the appointed goal: and there to hold and defend the territory gained: and to gather in the form of prisoners, guns and stores, the fruits of victory . . .'

Monash was now looking for a proving ground on which to demonstrate the validity of his theories of war. He chose the ridge which ran north from Villers-Bretonneux, about eight miles east of Amiens, to the River Somme. This ridge was dominated by the shattered village of Hamel, which – with Vaire Wood a little to the south – had been captured by the Germans on 4th April. From the ruined walls of Hamel, German artillery observers had good views over the Australian positions north of the Somme. It was a galling little dent in the British line. Monash decided to remove it.

During June, he submitted to Rawlinson a comprehensive plan for the recapture of Hamel. It was to be a battle in the new, Monash mould: he insisted that the plan depended entirely upon 'being supplied with the assistance of tanks, a small increase of my artillery, and an addition to my air resources . . . The operation will be primarily a tank operation . . . designed on lines to permit of the tanks effecting the capture of the ground: the roles of the infantry following the tanks will be (1) to assist in reducing strongpoints and localities (2) to mop up (3) to consolidate the

Lieutenant-General John Monash, commander of the Australian Corps

ground captured...'

Monash faced two problems in his eagerness to use the tanks. First, the army commander, Rawlinson, was cool towards the new machines, having been far from impressed by their unproductive *début* on the Somme two years earlier. However, Rawlinson had learned a lot about mental flexibility since the days of that terrible July, and as the plan unfolded he became no less eager than Monash to make use of the available armour.

The second problem, however, was more formidable. The Australian troops loathed and distrusted tanks. These emotions could be traced back to a muddy, bloody day in April 1917, when tanks were ordered to support an Australian infantry brigade forward at Bullecourt. The tanks were delayed by bad weather and ground conditions on their approach march, and when some finally arrived they proved sadly vulnerable targets as they advanced over the snow. The Australian brigade put in an abortive and insufficiently-supported attack, losing 2,250 officers and men out of a strength of 3,000. It was a bold man who praised tanks to the Australians after that.

It was particularly unfortunate that the Australian 4th Division, which Monash had chosen to play the major part in the coming battle of Hamel, was

**Tank-infantry battle rehearsal
complete with smokescreen,
Sautrecourt, 12th July 1918**

the parent unit of the brigade which had suffered so cruelly at Bullecourt. Monash was well aware of the problem.

'On the principle of restoring the nerves of the unseated rider by re-mounting him to continue the hunt,' he wrote later, 'it was especially important to wean the 4th Division from their prejudices...'

Rawlinson was equally aware of the problem. He visited the Australian Corps on 18th June, and talked to Major-General Sinclair MacLagan, who commanded the 4th Division, recording in his diary later that 'Mac-Lagan is not overjoyed at the prospect of tanks, but we will get him round when he has had experience of the new type...'

This new type was known as the Mark V. It was now reaching France at the rate of about fifty a week. The Mark V was a considerable improvement on the Mark IV. It could be driven and steered by one man, instead of three, as previously, and it was faster, with better handling qualities over rough ground. The armour had been thickened, and the male version mounted two improved versions of the 6-pounder gun, and four Hotch-

The armoured advance: Mark V tanks at
Bellicourt, September 1918

kiss machine guns. The female version carried five machine guns.

The tank unit chosen for the assault was the 5th Tank Brigade, commanded by Brigadier-General A Courage, a former cavalryman of the 15th Hussars. He had four companies of fighting tanks under command. This was a total of sixty machines – all of them the new Mark Vs. These tanks were to be accompanied into action by about 7,500 Australian infantry – mainly from the 4th Division, with some reinforcement from the 11th Brigade of the 3rd Division. In addition, four companies from the United States 33rd Division, looking for battle experience on the Western Front, were detailed to accompany the British tanks and Australian infantry into the attack. There existed already a strange kinship between the Americans and the Australians. An Australian newspaper correspondent, who visited the 33rd Division in training, had already recorded:

'We felt today as though we had been walking among ghosts. Wherever one goes one is struck more by the likeness of these men, amongst whom we have been moving, to the men of the old 1st Australian Division at Mena Camp and behind the lines in Gallipoli ... the swing of them, and the make up of the men, and the independent look upon their faces ...'

The Americans were a welcome addition to the scanty number of infantry with which Monash proposed to make the attack. A glance at his plan shows clearly that Hamel was to be uncompromisingly a tank operation. If the tanks failed, all would fail. In terms of manpower alone, Hamel would be a revolutionary battle.

By normal standards, his infantry strength was dangerously low. He was using six battalions on a front of 6,000 yards – compared with a normal frontage for such a force of between 1,200 and 2,000 yards. His artillery support was a little better – about 320 field guns or howitzers, and 313 heavier pieces. This gave him an 18-pounder

gun to every 25 yards of active front – and even this was only roughly half the power of a typical barrage of Third Ypres in the previous year.

Meanwhile, the process of weaning the Australian 4th Division from its prejudices began. The exercises in tank-infantry cooperation which now took place were more comprehensive than any yet seen on the Western Front – and bore a remarkable resemblance to the techniques practised in the British army during the later years of the Second World War.

Courage's tanks were now parked at Vaux, a village near Amiens. Busload after busload of Australian infantry was brought to the tank area, to climb all over the Mark Vs, make lurching journeys in their hot interiors, argue, smoke and drink with the British crews, and also rehearse the details of the coming battle. After this considerable effort in public relations, the Australian infantry had at least been persuaded to suspend judgment on the value of the tanks, but it was clear that only actual performance would finally allay suspicion. Courage himself was well aware of this. The orders issued to the tank battalions reflected his concern. They read, in part:

'It is the primary duty of the tanks to save casualties to the Australian infantry, and this cannot be done so long as tanks remain in rear of them. Tank commanders must do their utmost to get in between the infantry and the barrage wherever possible ...'

Paradoxically, it was the Australian infantry commanders themselves who did much to try to inhibit this policy. The tanks were nearly nine feet high, and it was always a danger that they might be struck by low-trajectory shells of the usual creeping barrage laid down by Australian guns in front of the advancing infantry. Thus the tank commanders were eager to take on the whole responsibility for fire support, and to dispense altogether with the creeping barrage, giving the tanks a free hand. Among the Australians, however, Bullecourt was still

ominous in memory. They demanded the barrage, so that they would not have to rely entirely on the tanks. Monash conceded the point, and the British tank commanders, eager to prove themselves and their machines in the coming battle, also gave way.

Monash now set about constructing the sort of clockwork battle which his theories demanded. He summed up his beliefs later by saying that 'in a well-planned battle . . . nothing happens, nothing can happen, except the regular progress of the advance according to the plan arranged. The whole battle sweeps forward relentlessly and methodically across the ground until it reaches the line laid down for the final objective . . .'

Few battles in the First World War can have been as well understood by those who were about to take part. Conference after conference between the various arms took place. The whole process of explanation went down from brigade, battalion and company commanders to platoons and

Armstrong Whitworth FK 8 biplanes gave the tanks excellent air support at Hamel Wood

sections. NCOs were issued with marked-up air reconnaissance photographs of the Hamel area, and every man carried a map of the battlefield with a message form on the reverse side.

Monash proposed to use aircraft as much as possible to help his infantry and tanks. He had excellent air support for such a limited operation. The tanks were given No 8 Squadron RAF – equipped with Armstrong Whitworth FK 8 biplanes – as their support squadron, while the Australian infantryhad their own squadron, III Australian Flying Corps, which flew RE 8 biplanes. In addition, he was able to call upon several other squadrons before and during the battle.

One of these was No 9 Squadron, RAF. Its RE 8s were to sling boxes in their bomb racks, and parachute machine gun ammunition forward

General von der Marwitz, commander of the German Second Army opposite Hamel

General John J Pershing, the American commander in France. He strove unsuccessfully to prevent the use of American troops at Hamel

into the advancing front line, where the dropping points were to be marked with V-shaped indicators made of white cloth. An additional burden would be removed from the infantry's backs by using four supply tanks to bring up wire, water, and bombs.

On the other side of the hill, the Germans waited, unknowing. The ridge was in the sector of General von der Marwitz's Second Army, which was part of Prince Rupprecht's Army Group. Hamel and Vaire Wood were held by four regiments (each of roughly British brigade strength) of the 13th Infantry and 43rd Reserve Division. The former division was thought by British Intelligence to be of good quality, but the 43rd was one of the units said to be fit 'for trench warfare only', of which Marwitz had recently been complaining to Ludendorff.

The date set by Monash for the attack was 4th July, American Independence Day. This was intended as a compliment to the four American companies – which between them totalled about 1,000 men – but there was nearly an unfortunate sequel. About twelve hours before zero, the American commander in France, General John Pershing, visited the battle zone and learned for the first time of the proposal to use American troops in the attack. He was strongly against it. He had for months been struggling hard to persuade Allied leaders, both military and political, that American troops must fight as an American army on an American front – not parcelled out in small units to stiffen the depleted ranks of British or French armies. Only in emergency, he had ordered, could Americans be used in small 'packets' in this way. He looked at the Hamel plan and decided – reasonably enough – that this could not be classed as an emergency. The Americans, he said, must be withdrawn.

Monash was furious. The removal of the Americans would take a vital cog from his battle machine. He turned at once to the ever-helpful Rawlinson,

Troops of the Australian 4th Division bivouac after their capture of Hamel Wood, August 1918

and asked him to ignore the order, saying that it was too late to take away the Americans, and that without them the attack could not take place. He further warned that if the Americans were withdrawn, 'no Australian would ever fight beside an American again . . .'

A war correspondent reported later: 'Rawlinson was very upset. He wanted the fight to go on (he said) "you don't realise what it means. Do you want me to run the risk of being sent back to England? Do you mean it is worth that?" "Yes, I do," said Monash. "It is more important to keep the confidence of the Americans and Australians in each other than to preserve even an army commander".'

Rawlinson rose to the occasion. 'It was too late to withdraw them, and I am afraid I had to disobey the order', he wrote coolly to a friend a day or so later.

Few of those who took part in the comparatively small struggle that was to follow can have had any inkling that it was, in its way, a turning point of the First World War. Still less would they have dreamed that it was also a turning point of war itself – that after Hamel war would never be quite the same. No action in history was more important for the tank; if the tanks had failed at Hamel, as they might well have failed, the whole cause of armour on the Western Front would have been put back for months or even longer. The consequences in the summer of 1918 might have been disastrous. On the night of 3rd July, without knowing it, a few thousands of Australians, Americans and British waited to make an indelible mark on the history of battle.

The assault at Hamel

It was a quiet, still night, but on the Allied side of the line it was a busy one. Zero hour was set for 3.10am. The troops ate their normal evening meal, and had another hot meal at midnight. At 10.30pm the tanks began to move up. They had roughly a mile to cover to reach the jumping-off points behind the front, and they moved at half-throttle to make as little noise as possible. At the same time, the FE 2B bombers of No 101 Squadron RAF lumbered overhead, drowning the throb of the tank engines, and dropping 350 25-lb bombs into the German reserve areas, in what must have seemed to the German command to be no more than an unusually sharp nuisance raid.

The battlefield ahead of the infantry was mostly grassland, open and rolling, with some areas of waist-high crops. The German defences in front of

FE 2B bombers of No 101 Squadron bombed the German reserve areas on the first day

Hamel and Vaire Wood consisted of only one main trench line, with not overmuch wire, though the village and wood themselves were known to contain many strong-points.

In front of this objective the preparations for Monash's clockwork battle proceeded smoothly. The tanks, as they reached their positions just behind the front, were met in the darkness by infantrymen who laid out tapes to act as guidelines to the assault positions of the infantry battalions. More infantry were out ahead of the Australian positions, quietly cutting paths through their own wire, while further guiding tapes were laid to lead the attack out into No-Man's Land. Shortly before 2am, moving like shadows, the successive waves of infantry slipped silently into place, and settled down to snatch a little sleep. One American account conveys their feelings, which were the usual soldier's mixture of apprehension and fatalism:

'As we were lined up with our bay-

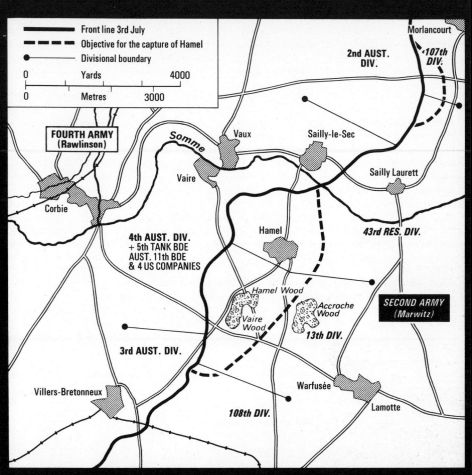

Legend

- **▬▬▬** Front line 3rd July
- **▬ ▬ ▬** Objective for the capture of Hamel
- **●▬** Divisional boundary

| Yards | 0 — 4000 |
| Metres | 0 — 3000 |

FOURTH ARMY
(Rawlinson)

Morlancourt

2nd AUST. DIV.

107th DIV.

Somme

Vaux

Sailly-le-Sec

Vaire

Sailly Laurett

Corbie

4th AUST. DIV.
+ 5th TANK BDE
AUST. 11th BDE
& 4 US COMPANIES

Hamel

43rd RES. DIV.

Hamel Wood

Accroche Wood

SECOND ARMY
(Marwitz)

Vaire Wood

13th DIV.

3rd AUST. DIV.

Warfusée

Villers-Bretonneux

Lamotte

108th DIV.

The situation before Monash's attack on Hamel: 4th July 1918

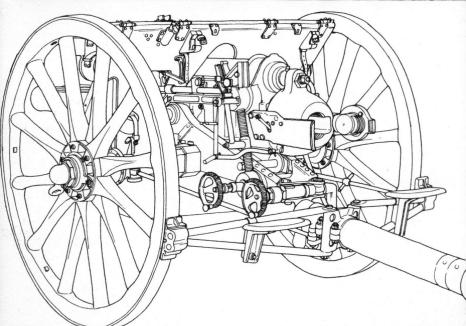

An excellent gun of its type, the British 18-pounder was easily moved, accurate and well-liked by its crews. *Calibre:* 3.3-inches. *Barrel length:* 28 calibres. *Weight of shell:* 18 pounds. *Weight of gun and carriage:* 3,800 pounds. *Range:* 7,000 yards. *Elevation:* —5° to +16°

An Australian 18-pounder in action out in the open

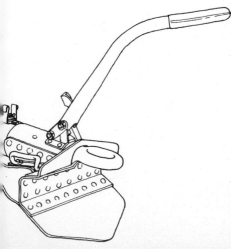

onets fixed, we all felt nervous . . . but when we reached our position, we took our places, lay down and soon forgot we were to go over the top . . . We were soon asleep . . .'

At 3.2am the Australian guns started their normal pre-dawn harassing fire. At the same instant, their noise drowned in German ears by the crump of the shell explosions, the tanks began to move up. Careful rehearsal had shown that it would take them exactly twelve minutes to reach the infantry. At the 3.10 zero, Monash's guns spoke in a single mighty clap of sound, and a storm of shells struck the German line in front of Hamel. Four minutes later the tanks arrived beside the infantry, and at the same moment, the carpet of explosive and smoke which covered No-Man's Land moved forward, allowing the tanks and infantry to begin their advance. Lighting their cigarettes, slinging their rifles, the Australians and Americans trudged out into the open. The artillery impressed them by its precision. An American officer wrote later:

'The barrage was most wonderful. The falling shells of the 18-pounders, exploding as they hit the ground, formed an almost straight line from the north edge of the action at the Somme to as far south as we could see . . . '

However, the gunners, in view of the need to conceal the impending attack, had not been able to range accurately, and had planned the barrage almost entirely from maps. Thus one or two guns fired a little short. Two sections – one American, one Australian – were wiped out by their own shells as they waited for the barrage to lift.

It soon became apparent that hitches could occur even in a Monash battle. Something unforeseen now hampered both tanks and infantry: the dust raised by the barrage, mingled with the smoke already fired by the Australian artillery, caused some of the tanks to miss their way in the murk, and also left some parties of

49

infantry lost in the midst of the enemy wire. Behind the wire, the waiting German machine guns began to cut down the little groups of Australians and Americans who were filtering through. One Australian Lewis gunner, a Queenslander named Dalziel, killed the crew of one German machine gun post with a revolver – a feat for which he was awarded the Victoria Cross. Like a khaki tide, ebbing and surging round the German wire, the Australians and Americans began to close with the main Hamel positions, though not without some considerable loss. The enemy, too, were losing men. Entering a trench near the sunken road in front of Hamel, an American officer, Captain GH Mallon (later to win the Medal of Honor) noted later: 'I counted about 40 German dead in a very small sector.'

Now, however, the sky was brightening over the Somme. In the dawn

British infantry go over the top

light, the floundering tanks began to move more purposefully, looming up beside the infantry in the dust and smoke. The infantry formed round them in small, improvised battle groups as they rumbled forward on to the German machine gun nests, pivoting on their broad tracks and often crushing the terrified crews into the standing corn.

In general, the Australians noted that the Germans showed considerable courage and tenacity in sticking to their positions until wiped out by the tanks – especially the crews of a new weapon, a large anti-tank rifle mounted on a bipod, which was encountered in small numbers for the first time.

In the full light of morning, the early difficulties in cooperation between the infantry and the tanks melted away. All along the edge of the covering barrage the tanks moved confidently, while the infantry called on them wherever a strong-point or a

machine gun post offered a problem – a problem which in previous battles would have meant the loss of many men. The Australian Official History describes a typical incident, after a platoon was fired on by a machine gun at the north edge of Hamel village:

'The platoon sergeant went to a tank and pulled the bell-handle at the back of the machine. A door opened, and he showed where the machine gun was. The tank . . . went straight over and rubbed it out . . . '

The infantry now lapped all round Hamel, and both the forward battalions of the German 202nd Reserve Rifle Regiment, inside the village itself, were overrun. The German command, indeed, had been staggered by the pace and nature of the attack. The forward infantry regiment of the German 13th Infantry Division had ceased to exist as a coherent force within the first few minutes. Only one officer and twenty men, apart from the battalion headquarters, returned

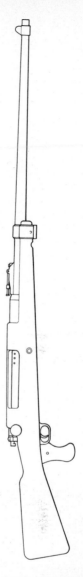

The introduction of the Mark I tank by the British in 1916 lead to the Germans producing an anti-tank rifle capable of penetrating the light armour of the early British tanks. This was a single-shot bolt-action rifle of 13mm calibre, which was fired from a tripod. The rifle weighed 36lbs and had a length of 5 feet 7 inches. Unfortunately for the Germans, however, the rifle proved to have too great a recoil to enable it to be an effective weapon

Above: German prisoners are moved back from Hamel. *Below:* Mopping up in Hamel village after a resounding tank-led victory

from its shattered positions. This headquarters was commanded by Cavalry Captain Freiherr von Preuschen. He later gave an account of the action from the German point of view:

'First, at 3am came drumfire. Only a quarter of an hour later headquarters heard in the direction of the front strong infantry fire. Soon after, tanks appeared on the Roman road (1,000 yards to the south) and the area north of it . . . When, at 5am "English" infantry was visible ahead, battalion headquarters knew that its companies had been overrun . . .'

The Australians were now within a couple of hundred yards of where von Preuschen and his staff crouched in their trench. The German commander withdrew the remnant of his force, crawling away over the open ground. The battle of Hamel, to all intents and purposes, was finished. The Australian infantry consolidated their gains, while here and there a tank moved to and fro, rubbing out some last defiant machine gun nest. From the small heights above the Somme, an observer noted: '4.45. Tanks everywhere beyond Hamel. Beyond Vaire Wood . . .'

The mechanical supply forces now began their operations. The RE 8 biplanes of No 8 Squadron zoomed over at under 1,000 feet, parachuting down a total of ninety-three boxes of ammunition to the Australians' forward machine gun positions. Even more dramatic, however, was the contribution made by the four tanks detailed as carriers. Each delivered to the infantry 124 coils of wire, 300 short-screw and 130 long-screw picquets, 150 Stokes bombs, 45 sheets of corrugated iron, 10,000 rounds of small-arms ammunition, 100 gallons of water – and a little whisky. The total load in the four tanks would have required an infantry carrying party of 1,200 men. The crews of the tanks added up to 24.

Monash was well satisfied with what had been virtually a demonstration battle. He said later:

'No battle within my previous experience passed off so smoothly, so exactly to timetable, or was so free from any kind of hitch. It was all over in ninety-three minutes. It was the perfection of team work. It attained all its objectives; and it yielded great results . . . The tanks fulfilled every expectation . . .'

By the standards of the Western Front, the casualties on the Allied side were very light when measured against the ground gained. The Australians lost, in dead and wounded, 51 officers and 724 men; the Americans 6 officers and 128 men. In both lists, however, many of the casualties were only walking-wounded cases. An unknown, but considerable number of Germans had been killed; in addition, more than 1,400 were taken prisoner, with 2 field guns, 41 trench mortars, and 171 machine guns. Five British tanks were lost – one of them to a chance hit by their own covering barrage. Thirteen tank men were wounded, but not one was killed. More important than all this, perhaps, was the fact that the Australians' confidence in tanks was now fully restored. It was a confidence which also began to permeate the higher command. The chief staff officer of the Tank Corps, Fuller, trenchantly summed up the change of mood after 4th July.

'In rapidity, brevity, and completeness of success, no battle of the war can compare with Hamel. The lessons we learned were all-important . . . Not in what it accomplished – the capture of a few square miles of ground and 1,506 prisoners – is to be sought the value of this battle, but, instead, in the realisation of the idea underlying it. Now we, or rather they who had stood outside our ranks, began to see clearly that it was all a matter of common sense – of a steel plate stopping a bullet. This was the decisive turning point in our tactics, and from 4th July onwards there was no question of who would or could win the war on land – the philosopher's stone was ours . . .'

Ludendorff's last bid

If, to the Allies, Hamel was a portent, to Ludendorff it can have seemed no more than a pinprick. He was now occupied with a much vaster canvas, on which he was already sketching the plan for Germany's last serious bid to win the war. He was also acutely aware that time was no longer on his side. The Americans were arriving in France in greater and greater numbers – a seemingly inexhaustible reserve of fit, willing young men to stiffen the tired armies on one side and cast despair into the minds of their foes. Foch, who had taken over the supreme command in March, was told then that there would be thirty-four American divisions in France by August; he had greeted the news by calling at once for 'up to 100'. Sifting the Intelligence estimates available on the other side of the hill, Ludendorff knew he must strike again – and quickly.

At first he turned his eyes to the British front in Flanders, reasoning – possibly correctly – that if this could be broken, the Allies would have little further heart for the war. Finally, however, he rejected the idea, explaining later:

'Again and again our thoughts returned to the idea of an offensive in Flanders. Strong English reserves were still assembled there, even after the French reserves had been withdrawn . . . an offensive at this point presented too difficult a problem. There were hopes that if an offensive at Rheims succeeded, there would be a very definite weakening of the enemy in Flanders . . .'

He now proposed to attack the French on either side of Rheims, along a line nearly forty-five miles long, and using a total of fifty-two divisions. He intended that the terrible threat to Paris, should this attack succeed, would suck in the Allied reserves in front of the capital, giving Rupprecht in Flanders the chance to strike a decisive blow against the British.

Ludendorff's new attack was given a

General Erich von Ludendorff, Germany's master strategist

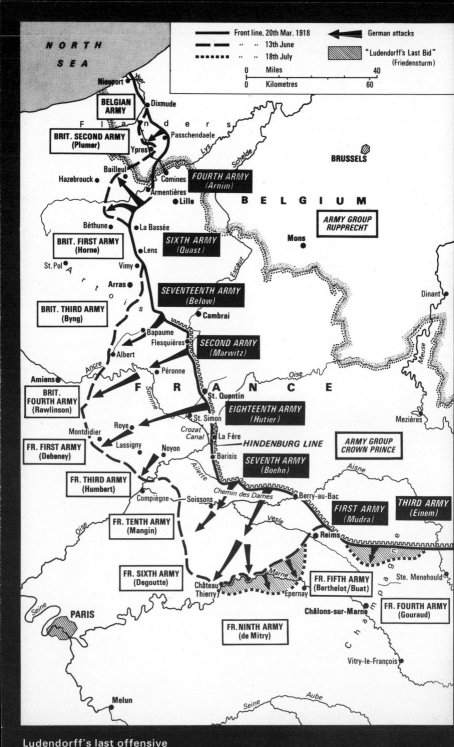

Ludendorff's last offensive

significant code-name. He called it *Friedensturm* – the Peace Offensive – a title which carried a built-in indication that mentally the German commander was already beginning to see it as a last throw. Although it was prepared in some respects with awesome Teutonic meticulousness, it completely lacked the vital element of surprise. Ludendorff himself said after the war that for days before the battle, its imminence was being freely discussed all over Germany. Bit by bit, the information leaked to the French command – in such detail, in fact, that although Foch was convinced that the attack was coming at Rheims, Haig was inclined to believe that Ludendorff intended to deceive the French by attacking on a comparatively small scale at Rheims, reserving the main blow for the British front in Flanders.

For once, Haig and his political masters, Lloyd George and the War Cabinet, were in agreement, as was illustrated by a comical little episode on 15th July. A telephone message arrived from General Sir Henry Wilson, the Chief of the Imperial General Staff, to say that the 'War Cabinet . . . discussed Foch's orders for moving British reserves to east of France. They feel anxiety that Rupprecht has large reserves left and will attack the British front, and it is directed "that if you consider the British army is endangered or if you think that General Foch is not acting solely on military considerations, they [the War Cabinet] rely on the exercise of your judgement . . . as to the security of the British front after the removal of these troops . . ." '

To Haig, who had already suffered Lloyd George's eagerness to curtail his powers, this message carried a certain irony. The politicians, as usual, wanted to have it both ways. Haig confided to his diary:

'I note that the government now tell me "to use my judgment" in obeying *orders* given me by the Generalissimo of the Allied armies. On 7th June at the Conference in Paris of the S of S for War with Foch and Clemenceau, we were confronted by a similar concrete case, and I put the definite question: "If General Foch orders me to move my reserves S of the Somme, is it permissible for me to delay to carry out F's orders until I have referred to the British government?" Foch objected and said he could not be Generalissimo on such terms. And so I was directed to obey all his orders at once, and notify War Cabinet if I took exception to any of them. On the other hand, Milner's [Milner was Secretary of State for War] instructions to me dated 22nd June, 1918, lay down: "You will carry out loyally any instructions issued to you by the C in C Allied Forces. At the same time, if any order given by him appears to imperil the British army, you should appeal to the British government before executing such order." This is a case of "heads you win and tails I lose." If things go well, the government take credit to themselves and the Generalissimo; if badly, the Field-Marshal will be blamed . . .'

However, on the same day that he made this diary entry, Haig went to meet Foch at Mouchy-le-Chatel, and learned that the German blow had fallen, as Foch had predicted, on the French armies both east and west of Rheims. He still seems to have felt that the main thrust could yet be made at the British front in Flanders, but under Foch's urgent request agreed to send two more divisions to help the French. 'Foch was in the best of spirits', he noted that evening.

There was good reason for the Generalissimo's elation. The German attack, east of Rheims at any rate, had developed in exactly the way that the French command had anticipated, and twenty-two German divisions had rushed headlong into a trap. A glance at the French dispositions to receive the *Friedensturm* tells the story. West of Rheims waited the French Tenth Army, under General Charles Mangin, and the Sixth, under De-

General Foch, Supreme Allied
Commander

General Berthelot, commander of
French Fifth Army

General Charles Mangin, commander of
French Tenth Army

General Gouraud, commander of
French Fourth Army

The A7V with its crew of fourteen, Germany's answer to the British Mark I

goutte. East of the city were positioned the French Fifth Army, under Berthelot, and the Fourth, commanded by Gouraud. It was to these men, and especially to Gouraud, that Pétain, commanding the French forces, had put forward his new ideas of elastic defence. Pétain – 'that cool, unemotional company director of modern war', as Liddell Hart once called him – had followed the disastrous Nivelle as French Commander-in-Chief. Of all the principles of war, the one called 'economy of force' weighed most heavily with him. He had worked tirelessly to rebuild the French army, both in men and morale, after the slaughter of Nivelle's pointless offensives in 1917. Now he had worked out a method of luring the Germans into a killing ground where they would be cut to pieces from a distance by French artillery, while they were effectively out of range for support from their own. This plan involved giving ground to the first wave of the German attack – and this, in itself,

was anathema to some French commanders for whom the loss of a couple of hundred yards of France constituted a major defeat. It was, indeed, as well that the first part of Pétain's plan depended mostly upon the intelligent Gouraud rather than the ferocious Mangin, whose passion for the offensive had already once cost him his command, but who was now back in the saddle at a moment when his instinct to attack might yield better results.

East of Rheims, the Germans attacked into an area where they found themselves increasingly bewildered. Only scattered outposts held what Ludendorff had imagined to be a strongly-defended trench system. The German creeping barrage passed over empty, deserted ground. Twenty tanks accompanied them into action – fourteen of the great slab-sided A7V

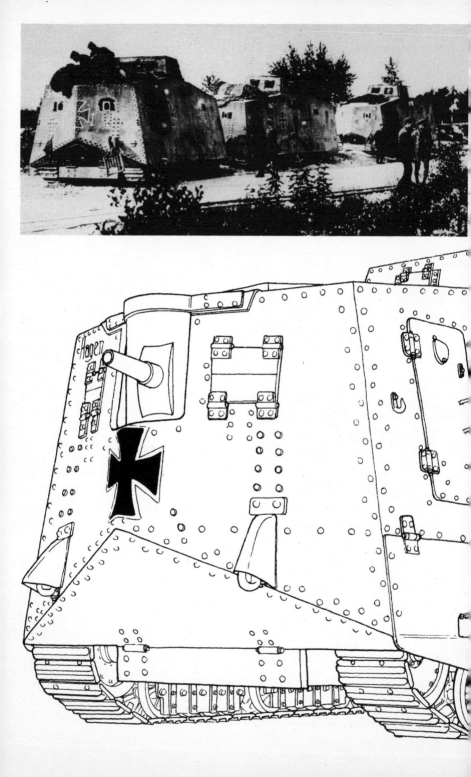

The A7V was Germany's first successful tank design, the prototype of which made its first trial at the end of April 1917. It was not, however, as good as British designs, as it was considered to be an infantry support weapon, and thus had inferior mobility and cross country performance compared with the British tanks, which were considered more in the light of cavalry. Only about 20 A7Vs were completed. *Weight:* 33 tons in action. *Crew:* 18 (commander, driver, gunner, loader, two engineers and six machine gun crews of two men each). *Length:* 26 feet 3 inches. *Height:* 10 feet 10 inches. *Width:* 10 feet 0½ inches. *Armament:* One Sokol 57mm gun and six (on early models seven) LMG '08 machine guns with up to 500 rounds and 36,000 rounds of ammunition respectively. *Armour:* Front 30mm, rear 20mm and sides 15mm. *Power:* Two Daimler-Benz water-cooled inlines, 100hp each. *Speed:* 8 mph on roads, 4 mph cross country. *Trench crossing:* 7 feet. *Step:* 1 foot 7 inches. *Range:* 60 miles

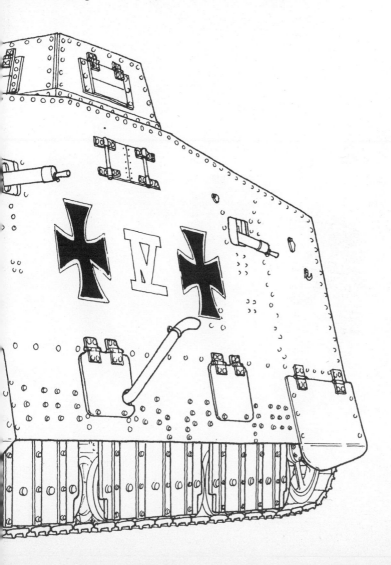

German tanks lumber into action

Above: A captured Mark IV in German hands. Below: Well-equipped with gas masks, a German transport column in 1918

machines which German engineers
had finally produced as an answer to
the British Mark I, and six captured
British machines. This pathetic total
– all of which were destroyed in the
next few hours by the French guns –
was the only feature of the *Friedensturm* which in any way distinguished
the technique of the assault from the
methods of the immediate past.
However, though the methods were
much as before, the results were not.
The Germans were beating furiously
at the air, and as they flailed forward
against a mere handful of machine
gun posts, they passed rapidly beyond
their own covering barrage and into
the carefully-planned target areas of
the French artillery, massed, with
the waiting, untouched French infantry, along a carefully prepared
line. A young German officer recorded
sadly:

'I have lived through the most
disheartening day of the whole war . . .
This wilderness of chalk is not very
big, but it seems endless when one gets
held up in it, and we are held up . . .
No shade, no paths, not even roads;
just crumbling white streaks on a
flat plate. Across this wind rusty
snakes of barbed wire. Into this the
French deliberately lured us. They put
up no resistance in front: they had
neither infantry nor artillery in this
forward battle zone. Our guns bom-
barded empty trenches; our gas shells
gassed empty artillery positions;
only in little hidden folds of the
ground, sparsely distributed, lay
machine gun posts like lice in the
seams and folds of a garment, to give
the attacking forces a warm recep-
tion. After uninterrupted fighting
from five a.m. until the night, smoth-
ered all the time with carefully-
directed fire, we succeeded in advancing only about three kilometres . . .
We did not see a single dead French-
man, let alone a captured gun or
machine gun, and we suffered heavy
losses . . .'

At the end of the day, the assaulting
German First and Third Armies had

German troops await a French attack near Soissons

gained nothing. It was a decisive check, and the losses were too heavy to allow of a new assault upon the untouched French positions. Wearily, by midday on the 16th, Ludendorff ordered the *Friedensturm*, for the twenty-two divisions east of Rheims, to cease.

To the west of the city, from the German point of view, the situation at first seemed much more promising. The technique of the German attack, as against Gouraud, might be familiar, but its execution was awesome in its relentless ferocity. The German waves swept ominously forward, across the River Marne, and formed a dangerous bridgehead on its farther bank, driving on for nearly six miles. Paris was less than sixty miles away. Winston Churchill, in a typical bravura passage, captured the essence of this last, bloody spasm of a dying form of war:

'Down from beyond the German parapets leaped the cataracts of fire and steel. Forward the indomitable veterans of the Fatherland. It is the Marne that must be crossed. Thousands of cannon and machine guns

General Pétain

lash its waters into foam. But the shock troops go forward, war-worn, war-hardened, and once again *Nach Paris* is on their lips. Launching frail pontoons and rafts in a whistling, screaming crashing hell, they cross the river, mount the farther bank, grapple with the French; grapple also with the Americans – numerous, fresh and coolly handled. After heavy losses they drive them back, and make good their lodgements. They throw their bridges, drag across guns and shells, and when night falls upon the bloody field, 50,000 Germans have dug themselves in on a broad front four miles beyond the Marne. Here they stop to gather strength after performing all that soldiers have ever done . . . '

Stopping to gather strength, however, was fatal. The failure of the German divisions opposite Gouraud inhibited Ludendorff from encouraging those in the Marne bridgehead from trying to push farther south, into an even more vulnerable salient. On the French side, Pétain's reaction was intelligent, but perhaps overcautious. He had planned a three-phase reaction to the German offensive: first, to contain it; second, to strike at the flanks of the pockets on each side of Rheims; third, to push Mangin's Tenth Army east across the rear of the whole enemy salient, with the intention of trapping the German armies inside the bag of ground they had won at such considerable cost.

However, the German success in crossing the Marne had disturbed him more than it had encouraged Ludendorff. Pétain now planned to put more punch into his second phase – the flank blows – and to withdraw the necessary forces from Mangin, postponing the vital third phase accordingly. This policy, had it been followed would have mauled the German

Above: The German advance to the Marne continues. *Below:* French Renault tanks rally after an attack near Grisolles on the Aisne. *Above right:* German shells fall on American lines near Château Thierry, 20th July 1918

advance without inflicting a major defeat.

The plan did not at all appeal to Foch. The Generalissimo was nothing if not an opportunist, and he seems to have sensed the weakness behind the impressive facade of the German salient. Moreover, at his meeting with Haig at Mouchy, he had firmly promised that Mangin would attack on time – an attack which would go some way to insure Haig against the risk he had taken of releasing British divisions from Flanders. Pétain's order was countermanded, and Mangin was instructed to attack at once. On the telephone to Pétain, Foch was imperious and emphatic, saying:

'There can be no question of slowing down, still less of stopping Mangin's preparations. In case of urgent, extreme need you may take troops absolutely indispensable, informing me at once . . . '

Foch's order meant that Pétain's second and third phases of the battle were now fused into one – that Mangin was to strike against the neck of the salient while the defensive battle was still going on far down in the bulge. Thus the one vital feature of Mangin's operation was surprise, giving him the chance to seal off the neck before Ludendorff was able to turn and strike at this new threat.

Against the usual experience in such operations on the Western Front, Mangin now achieved surprise, because he, too, had learned about armour. While the French and British air forces struck repeatedly at the Marne crossings, mauling and finally paralysing the German attempts to bring reinforcements and ammunition into the bridgehead, Tenth Army went into the attack. Mangin had ten divisions – including the American 1st and 2nd Divisions – in the first line; six divisions and Robillot's Cavalry Corps in the second line; and two British divisions – the 15th and 34th – in reserve. He also had 346 tanks, most of them the small, fast (by 1918 standards) Renault FTs.

Of this total, 225 finally got into action.

He used the tanks on the Cambrai model. At 4.35am on 18th July, without any artillery preparation, he launched his attack to the south of Soissons, making his immediate objective the seizing of the road to Château Thierry. Out of the concealing woods of the forests of Compiègne and Retz poured the little Renaults, causing consternation among the Germans as they moved in deadly spreading ripples through the thick, waist-high wheat.

'For the first time', Ludendorff reported, 'small low fast tanks that allowed the use of machine guns above the corn were used . . . the rapid movement of the numerous fast tanks in the high standing corn increased the effect of the surprise . . . '

The German discomfiture was further increased by the inadequacy of the hurriedly-constructed trench system in the Marne salient. With their minds concentrated on the anticipated drive to Paris, the Germans appear to have neglected the formidable rear defence lines against which the Allies had often bloodied a nose after an initial success. Mangin achieved a striking success, capturing 10,000 prisoners and 200 guns by the evening of this first day, which ended with the French artillery dominating the road to Château Thierry, forcing the Germans to begin to withdraw across the Marne.

However, Mangin's success could not in itself be transformed into a

German prisoners under American guard, Château Thierry

decisive result. The reason was simple: the impetus of the attack had been carried by the little Renault tanks, and they were neither battle-proof enough nor sufficiently adequate technically to sustain this role into the days that followed. The German gunners, when they stuck to their guns, took a heavy toll of them, and many also broke down during the first day. Mangin lost 102 tanks on 18th July, 50 on 19th July, and 17 (out of 32 in action) on 20th July. Nothing was left to hammer home the initial success. Mauled, battered, bleeding but still unbroken, the German assault divisions dragged themselves back across the river. The threat to Paris had been lifted; the German troops were becoming increasingly sick at heart; and after a spring of fear and anxiety, the Allies sensed the beginning of a summer of success. But the armoured breakthrough of 1918 had not yet taken place, and when it came, it would be bedevilled by some of the same problems that Mangin faced. Neverthelss, it was a victory – a victory of manoeuvre, made possible because for one day at least, the little French tanks had been adequate for their task. Mangin summed it up cheerfully after the battle: 'Marshal Foch conceived it. General Gouraud made it possible. Me, I did it . . . '

Planning the counterstroke

Mangin's success was especially cheering to the Allied command, since it fitted a more sanguine and optimistic change in their thinking about the coming summer. On 5th July, the day after Hamel, Rawlinson – now an enthusiastic convert to tank warfare – put forward to Haig a plan for Fourth Army to attack north and east of Amiens both to capture its important railway line and to put the city outside the range of ordinary German gunfire. As it happened, this was very much in line with the thinking of Foch – and it was not very long before Haig was persuaded to switch his gaze from Flanders to the possibility of successful efforts elsewhere. Haig had already seen that Mangin's success must have gravely inhibited the possibility of a sudden attack on the British positions further north. He wrote in his diary on 25th July:

'As we are fairly well prepared to meet an attack by Rupprecht upon my Second Army, it is most likely that the attack won't be delivered. So I am prepared to take the offensive and have approved of an operation taking place on Rawlinson's front, and steps have been taken to make preparations very secretly in order to be ready, should the battle now being fought out on the Marne cause the situation to turn in our favour . . . '

On the following day, Foch at his headquarters at the Château Bombon, near Melun, met Haig, Pershing and Pétain, the three Allied Commanders-in-Chief. His mind was firmly concentrated on a great counteroffensive, and the abortive German counterstroke over the Marne had played into his hands. Ironically, the ideas he now put forward reached back in essence to earlier German theories – those of Karl von Clausewitz, the 19th Century master of theoretical war. Clausewitz had written:

'The mere parrying of a blow is something contrary to the idea of

Crown-Prince Rupprecht of Bavaria

74

General Pershing

Marshal Foch

war, because warfare is unquestionably not passive endurance. If the defender has gained an important advantage, defence has done its part, and under protection of this advantage, he must return the blow if he does not want to expose himself to certain ruin . . . A swift and vigorous transition to attack – the flashing sword of vengeance – is the most brilliant point of the defensive . . . '

Foch himself was no Clausewitzian in the full sense of the term. '*Attaquez, attaquez*', was the principle to which he most closely clung. It was good fortune for the Allies that this slogan at last coincided with a time at which attack was not only eminently possible, but also eminently desirable. Foch was not, perhaps, a man for all seasons of war, nor for every hour of the great conflict that had now rolled bloodily on for almost four years. But this, for sure, was the hour, and in Foch the hour had found the man.

The blow he now proposed was intended to be of considerable, but not decisive, proportions. He wanted to free three vital stretches of railway from German interference: the Paris-Avricourt line near Château Thierry, the Paris-Amiens line in front of Amiens, and the Paris-Avricourt line near St Mihiel, in the general area of Verdun. These lines were of vital importance in any future major counter-offensive, since they ran laterally across the front, and were thus necessary for the swift transfer of troops from one sector of it to another. The meeting at the Château Bombon was in general agreement with these objectives, and four days later Foch issued the formal order for the first phase, which was the freeing of the Paris-Amiens line. The operation, however, was intended to go somewhat further than this limited objective, and Foch's order added that 'the offensive, covered in the north by the Somme, will be pushed as far as possible in the direction of Roye'. This left the whole plan somewhat open-ended, since

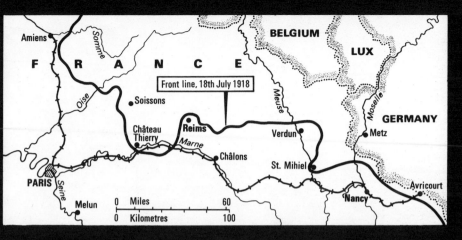

The vital railways

Above: American infantry of the 107th Infantry Regiment train with tanks near Beauquesnes, September 1918. *Below:* A Renault tank in the Bois de Reims, 24th July 1918

Roye lay more than five miles south-east of the old outer defence lines for Amiens, which were now held by German troops at the edge of the tide that had flowed west during the spring. This imprecision was to have a marked effect on the coming battle, because it left the door open for yet another escalation of the plan – an escalation which would begin to err on the side of over-optimism.

Meanwhile, however, Rawlinson and Fourth Army had good grounds for confidence. Monash's Australian Corps, by a policy of vigorous raiding had, even before Hamel, established a considerable moral ascendancy over the Germans opposite them. The German trenches captured at Hamel had proved to be poorly-dug and planned, and nothing like as formidable as the trench-lines of earlier years. The German divisions themselves were reckoned to be weak, with an average strength of about 3,000 men each. Moreover, the Spanish influenza which was prevalent on both sides of the line, was believed to be hitting the Germans, worse-fed and clothed than the Allies, more severely than their opposite numbers in Fourth Army. The very landscape in front of the Allied line seemed to beckon to tanks and cavalry. It was open, chalky, and undulating – and since it had not had months of heavy fighting, it was relatively unscarred by the pock-marks of shelling which disfigured the battlefields of the Somme. More important than all this, however, was the slow deterioration in German morale. The setback of July, and the discovery by German front-line troops of the increasing part played by the Americans in the war were having an insidious effect on German minds. A German staff officer who had advanced in July into the German bulge west of Rheims had written despondently on the 25th:

'The confusion and blunders are increasing . . . We have been spending uncomfortable days in crowded ruined villages, in which we were thrown hither and thither without plan, disturbed day and night by bombardment and bombing from somewhere or other. Today everything seems to be at a standstill. I do not believe that we shall ever get our hands free again. The American army is there – a million strong. That is too much . . . '

By 4th August, it all seemed to be getting worse, and he wrote:

'I have got a bad opinion of the situation; but when I express it I find that people shut their minds rather than their ears to what I have to say. The German officer cannot realise that things are as they are. Here are the indications. Everybody is tired of the war. One hears men say: "Why not give them this damned Alsace Lorraine?" This from men who are by no means the worst, even from the stoutest fighting men. Their manhood has been sapped in such a way that there is no stiffening it . . . Carelessness and callousness are spreading like plagues. One feels that the year from which for the first

General Debeney, commander of French First Army

time one seriously hoped for a decision, because there was no holding out any longer, has been simply thrown away . . . '

On the Allied side of the line there was also weariness and cynicism, but it was less in amount and also notably absent in certain vital areas of the military machine. Passchendaele and the Chemin des Dames had done something to blunt the ardour of both British and French infantry, but the tank troops of both armies were still enthusiastic and eager to prove their value. More important still, the Australians and Canadians had been less harshly handled during the German spring offensive than their British and French comrades, and they were still aggressively and efficiently cocky in their attitude to their foes. There was also the swelling American contingent, inexperienced but gravely and courteously willing to learn. Thus it will be seen that the battle of morale, at any rate, was going steadily in favour of the Allies. If this advantage was to be properly used, a battle must be devised which would do the maximum

to increase Allied morale, and to strike at the flagging spirits of the Germans. This is what Rawlinson, aided by Fuller of the tanks, now set out to do.

Foch intended that the battle should be a combined operation between Rawlinson's Fourth Army and General Debeney's French First Army, on the British right flank. Unity of command was essential, and Foch placed Debeney under British command. The main brunt of the offensive, however, was to be borne by Fourth Army; the role of Debeney was to guard the right flank, though his left-hand corps – the XXXI – would wheel roughly into line with the Fourth Army right.

The date set for the attack was 8th August. Only three days before this, to the consternation of the tank staff, the target was raised again. The objective now was dramatic but vague. Haig ordered Rawlinson to be prepared to make a major advance, noting to his diary:

'I thought that the Fourth Army orders aimed too much at getting a final objective on the old Amiens defence line, and stopping counterattacks on it. This is not far enough, in my opinion, if we succeed at the start in surprising the enemy. So I told Rawlinson . . . to advance as rapidly as possible and capture the old Amiens line of defence . . . and to put it into a state of defence; but not to delay; at once reserves must be pushed on to capture the line Chaulness-Roye. The general direction of the advance is to be on Ham . . . '

This instruction roughly doubled the extent of the planned advance, and the GHQ Operation Order of the same date emphasised that 'in the event of an initial success the battle will develop into one of considerable magnitude . . . ' In view of the German situation, Haig's intentions can be seen to be intelligent and far-sighted. However, the gradual escalation of the objectives had taken place in a haphazard way, without the benefit of

Above: Camouflaged in the corn near Albert, Mark V tanks of 10th Tank Battalion, 9th August 1918. *Below:* Mark V female tanks advance through Meaulte

a single driving intelligence. This was a lack which would reveal itself at vital moments in the coming days.

Rawlinson's outstanding characteristics as a soldier were his flexibility and his willingness to learn. He now made it plain that he had learned a great deal from Hamel. There had been a number of special conferences held by officers who had taken part in the 4th July attack, and two papers on the new Monash technique had been published by GHQ for the guidance of those about to launch the assault of 8th August. This, Rawlinson had decided, was to be Hamel ten times over.

As at Hamel, the infantry available was the smallest practicable force. It consisted of the British III Corps, with the 12th, 18th, 47th, and 58th Divisions in the line, and the American 33rd Division in reserve; the Canadian Corps, with the 2nd and 3rd Divisions in line, and the 1st and 4th. in reserve; and the Australian Corps, with the 2nd, 3rd and 4th Divisions in line, and the 1st and 5th in reserve. Also in reserve were the 1st, 2nd, and 3rd Divisions of the Cavalry Corps. The whole infantry and cavalry force was to be supported by the 3rd, 4th and 5th Brigades and the 10th Battalion of the Tank Corps – a total of more than 400 machines, the most formidable armoured striking force of the war. Air support, too, was on a considerable scale – six corps squadrons, eight fighter squadrons, and three RAF bomber squadrons.

Since Rawlinson intended to use the 47th Division in III Corps only as a flank guard, it will be seen that the entire infantry weight of the attack would be borne by only eight divisions. Moreover, his artillery support was no more than adequate. It consisted of 1,386 field guns and 684 heavy guns, which meant a field gun frontage of 29 yards and a heavy gun frontage of 59 yards. All, in fact, would again depend on the tanks, which were allotted to the infantry by Fuller.

A brigade each of Mark Vs was

Tank, Medium Mark A (Whippet). The medium, or cavalry, type of tank was developed in parallel with the heavier models to exploit any breakthrough effected by the latter. The Whippet was designed to be powered by two 45hp engines, one for each track. Steering was by throttling the engine on the inside of the desired turn, and opening up the other engine. This was a difficult system, and drivers needed a lot of practice. *Weight:* 14 tons. *Length:* 20 feet. *Height:* 9 feet. *Width:* 8 feet 7 inches. *Power:* Two Taylor 4-cylinder inlines, 45hp each. *Speed:* 8.3mph maximum. *Range:* 160 miles. *Armament:* 3 Hotchkiss machine guns with 5,400 rounds. *Armour:* 12mm maximum, 6mm minimum. *Crew:* 3

given to the Australian and Canadian Corps, and a battalion to III Corps. A tank brigade in August 1918 consisted of four tank battalions, each of 36 fighting tanks. Thus the Canadians and Australians got 144 tanks each, and the British III Corps 36. A further battalion was held in general reserve.

British army thinking about the role of tanks was both expanding and advancing, though a last desperate attempt was still being made – in spite of the unfortunate experience of Cambrai – to prove that tanks and cavalry could exploit together, the one in support of the other. The Mark V tank with a road speed of barely five miles an hour, was, of course, far too slow to cooperate with cavalry. A new type of tank had now been developed, with this in mind. It was called the Medium A, or Whippet, and it had an appearance quite different from the lozenge shape of the Marks I, IV, and V. It had a long low chassis, with a high cab at the rear. This was the fighting turret, with an armament of

A Whippet with a lone passenger

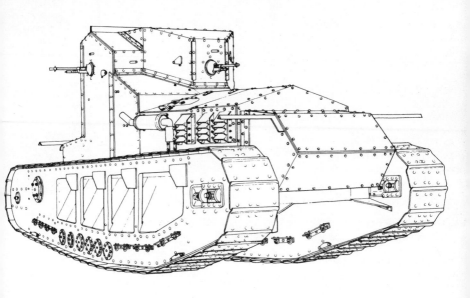

Whippets of 3rd Tank Battalion on 26th March 1918, the first day on which Whippets were in action

four Hotchkiss machine guns. The Whippet weighed fourteen tons and had a crew of three. Its speed on roads was nearly nine miles an hour, and it had an operating range of eighty miles, compared with thirty-five for the standard Mark IV. These characteristics, it was intended, would make it a suitable companion for the horse soldiers of the Cavalry Corps. Such plans, however, represented the triumph of hope over experience; the cavalry establishment, not unnaturally, still declined to believe that its role on the Western Front was vanishing. There were clearer heads in the tanks, as Fuller made clear at one of Rawlinson's battle conferences, when there was a discussion on how an initial breakthrough might be exploited, and how the cavalry – the traditional instrument of exploitation – might cooperate

with the Whippet tanks. Fuller totally opposed such cooperation, recording later:

'Personally, my opinion was that they could accomplish next to nothing, and that to attach two battalions of Medium A machines to them was an utter waste of good metal. I pointed out that tanks and horses could not cooperate together, because one was bullet-proof and the other was not . . . '

Instead, Fuller put forward a scheme of his own. He proposed that the ninety-six Whippets of the 3rd and 6th Tank Battalions would be kept in reserve until a breakthrough had been made by the infantry and heavier Mark Vs. They would then be put through the gap to make a wide and demoralising destructive sweep through the German artillery and service areas opposite Debeney's First French Army, eventually emerging back on to the Allied front south-east of Montdidier. He believed that if this was done, a gap of twenty miles would be torn in the German defences, which

also saw the possibilities of mechanical armoured cavalry as a destructive and disruptive force behind the German line. He had under command, in addition to his tank force, the 17th Armoured Car Battalion, equipped with 20mph cars armed with a Hotchkiss machine gun at front and rear. Twelve of the sixteen cars were sent to an Australian infantry division, but Monash kept four cars under his own hand. His orders for them read:

'These sections will be sent forward under the orders of the CO 17th Armoured Car Battalion, passing the green line as soon as practicable after Zero plus 4 hours, and proceeding eastward, following the lifts of our heavy artillery bombardment, so as to pass the blue line at or after Zero plus five hours.

'The area to be reconnoitered lies in the bend of the Somme, north of the Villers-Bretonneux-Chaulnes railway; but the old Somme battlefield lying NE of Chaulnes need not be entered.

'Information is required as to presence, distribution, and movement of enemy supporting and reserve troops, and his defensive organisations within this area.

'While the primary function of this detachment is to reconnoitre and not to fight, except defensively, advantage should be taken of every opportunity to damage the enemy's telephonic and telegraphic communications ...'

Ludendorff would be unable to block.

It was a bold plan, but it was undeniably chancy. Rawlinson considered it, but turned it down. Several considerations must have weighed with him: the Whippets were not heavily armed, and their mechanical reliability was still uncertain. Fuller himself thought that the plan was rejected 'because he [Rawlinson] did not trust the French to make good what the tanks might render possible ...' He added, defiantly: 'Though I realised that such an operation was a risky one, I held, and still do, that it was feasible and would have proved decisive.' One can understand Rawlinson's reservations about Fuller's plan, but in the event, a single Whippet tank, breaking through the German front, was to go far to vindicate Fuller's bold ideas, and also to fight, as we shall see, one of the greatest single-tank actions of history.

There was one other, besides Fuller, who gave evidence now of having glimpsed the future of warfare Monash

If there was one principle of war which weighed more heavily than the others with Rawlinson, it was that of surprise. His physical appearance and general background might well give the impression that he was a bluff British soldier of the 'ride straight at your fences' mould. Tall and elegant, he had a slightly receding chin and a military moustache. Those who opposed him on manoeuvres found, however, that he was not as simple a character as he appeared. The word in army circles went round: 'Rawly is a fox.' It was a reputation which he had little

British armoured car on patrol near Biefvillers

opportunity to vindicate in the bloodbath of the Somme, but he redeemed it now.

Secrecy was the whole basis of Rawlinson's plan, and it became a watchword for Fourth Army. It was not until 4th August that Rawlinson divulged his plans to his cavalry divisional and brigade commanders, although the high officers of the Australian and Canadian Corps were told, under pledge of complete secrecy, on 21st July. In the past, the careless movement of staff officers in the line had been known to give away the fact that an attack was impending, and the Fourth Army General Staff Instructions now strictly forbade the presence in the line of 'a large number of staff officers with maps looking over the parapet and visiting observation posts.' Instead, it was ordered that staff officers should do their reconnaissance in small parties,

limited to the absolute minimum practicable number.

Since, in the event, surprise was to play a decisive part in the coming attack, it is worth examining exactly in what way Rawlinson was attempting to deceive the German command. First, he had to convince them that the movement of the Canadian Corps from reserve, which was sure to be noted by enemy agents or air reconnaissance, was being made for quite different purposes. He decided to give the impression that the Canadians were intended to attack the key feature of Mont Kemmel, on the British Second Army front, which had fallen to the Germans during the spring offensive. Two Canadian battalions, two casualty clearing stations, and the Canadian wireless section were now moved into the Kemmel area, amid ostentatious but deliberately inefficient attempts at secrecy. The men themselves were not told that their role was illusory, and gradually the reports went back to the German High Command that the Canadians were preparing to attack Kemmel.

Rawlinson's real role for the Canadians, however, was to attack on the right centre of the Fourth Army line, which was being extended down as far as the Amiens-Roye road, running diagonally across the projected battlefield. The French now evacuated their trenches in this sector, in order to reinforce Debeney farther to the right, and a single Australian brigade quietly took over the sector. It was not proposed to move the Canadians into this part of the line until shortly before zero.

Inevitably, of course, many men, officers and NCOs gradually became aware of what was going on, especially in the administrative services which were organising the details of the whole vast operation. Rawlinson's plan, as we have seen, partly relied on deceiving Fourth Army itself, but could never be enough. Secrecy must, in the last resort, depend upon the steadiness, loyalty and common sense of a very large body of men. A little notice was issued to all ranks, and pasted in the 'small books' carried by every officer and man. It was headed 'Keep Your Mouth Shut', and it said:

'Do not talk. When you know that your unit is making preparations for an attack, don't talk about them to men in other units or to strangers, and keep your mouth shut, especially in public places. Do not be inquisitive about what other units are doing; if you hear or see anything, keep it to yourself. If you hear anyone else talking about operations, stop him at once ... If you should ever have the misfortune to be taken prisoner, don't give the enemy any information beyond your rank and name. In answer to all other questions you need only say "I cannot answer." He cannot compel you to give any other information. He may use threats. He will respect you if your courage, patriotism and self-control do not fail.

Every word you say may cause the death of one of your comrades ... '

To soldiers of the Second World War, such instructions were commonplace enough. In 1918 they were less common, especially on the German side of the line. At a vital point in the next few days, as we shall see, British soldiers who were taken prisoner heeded the urgings of this little leaflet, so that Rawlinson was able to maintain surprise. Compare this with the free discussion, all over Germany a month earlier, of Ludendorff's abortive *Friedensturm*, and it will be seen that the British obsession with secrecy was soundly based.

Staff officers, whose relative comfort under campaigning conditions was inevitably compared with the discomfort and even misery of life in the trenches, have earned a poor public image in the history of the First World War. Nevertheless, the coming battle was made possible only by a masterpiece of staffwork. The man chiefly responsible for this was Rawlinson's Chief of General Staff, Major-General Sir Archibald Montgomery. A few years later as Chief of the Imperial General Staff, Montgomery-Massingberd (the name he later adopted) was to have a stultifying influence upon the armoured development of the British army. In 1918, however, when the problem was the straightforward one of organising an offensive, he was eager, energetic, and brilliantly professional. The administrative arrangements for a battle in 1918 make formidable reading: those issued for Fourth Army on 4th August dealt with railways, railheads, roads, canals, ammunition, food supplies, water, ordnance, labour, medical services, cavalry remounts, veterinary services, traffic control, civilians, and prisoners of war. Ordinary working supplies alone ranged from the mediaeval to the ultra-modern. The Cavalry Corps, for instance, was issued with 480,000 lbs of oats and 48,000 iron rations; by contrast, the 4th Tank Brigade alone received

German troops advance

80,000 gallons of petrol, 4,000 gallons of engine oil, and 20,000 lbs of grease. About 50,000 containers of pea soup and Oxo were sent to the Australian Corps, with the cheering addition of 1,500 gallons of rum.

Meanwhile, moving at night, the troops were shuffled into position. About 300 special trains moved them to their sectors. Supplies came on lorries which moved with rope-bound wheels on sanded roads near the front to reduce the amount of noise the Germans could hear. When tanks moved, they moved in darkness, and low-flying planes were used to drown the rumble of their half-throttled engines. By the night of 7th August, the 100,000 men of the Canadian Corps were standing, ready, just behind their portion of the line, and the thousands of animals and men of the Cavalry Corps were concentrated in reserve. The question now for Rawlinson and his staff was: 'Do the Germans know?' Gradually it became apparent that, in spite of one or two alarms, they did not. They appeared, indeed, to exhibit a surprising complacency about the possibility of another tank attack.

This complacency is even more surprising since they were in fact receiving reports of troop movements which, though inaccurate in themselves, did give some indication of what was going to happen. For instance, on 3rd August, five days before the attack, the German Second Army reported nervously that its outposts could hear tanks on the move near Villers-Bretonneux, although in fact the tanks had not yet reached that area of the front. On 6th August, Rupprecht's Army Group actually issued an Intelligence report which said:

'Result of reconnaissance: about 100 tanks observed on the road Ailly-Moreuil . . . ' This was astonishingly prophetic, since Debeney's First Army in this sector was due to be reinforced by ninety machines. These machines, however, did not arrive there until the early hours of 8th August: the tanks the Germans 'saw' were phantoms from the future. Phantoms or not, however, they could have won Rupprecht valuable time had he acted on this false-true report. He remained indifferent. A German regimental officer commented wryly afterwards: 'Not even a request to keep a sharp look-out. We were anxious because anyone who brings up a hundred tanks is not planning a joy-ride ...'

The opponents of Rawlinson's Fourth Army in the coming attack would be General von der Marwitz's Second Army, which occupied almost exactly the proposed front of attack. Von der Marwitz had ten divisions in the line and four in reserve, but on 3rd August he had complained to Supreme Headquarters that only two divisions were fit for battle. Five, he said, were 'trench warfare only', three were fit only for defence on a quiet front, and three were in need of being relieved. Later German accounts give the rifle strength of the bat-

talions of a typical infantry regiment
of these divisions as 255, 286, and 404.
All the battalions were said to be
short of officers, and with long lists of
flu-stricken men.

The German defences marked the
edge of the German spring offensive.
They were not as formidable as those
of earlier years. Much of the wiring
was poor, and there was a general
shortage of good infantry shelters,
some of the earthworks being no
more than breast-high. However,
machine guns were everywhere – in
the angle of every trench, in scattered
shell-holes, and behind the tumbled
bricks of every smashed farm cottage.
There was going to be plenty for the
tanks to do.

On 5th August, there was an Allied
alarm. A German Württemberg Division raided the III Corps sector,
capturing about 200 officers and men.
The raid appears to have been a
morale-raising reprisal for a similar
raid carried out by the Australians,
just before they had handed over the
sector a few days before. The Australian raid had also been successful
but its timing had been ill-judged.
The result was that the Württemberg
Division seriously upset the III Corps
preparations for 8th August – an
upset which was to have serious
effects on the progress of the battle,
and would also, ironically enough,
eventually cost many Australian
lives. More important still, from the
point of view of the Fourth Army
staff, was the question of whether any
officer or man taken prisoner would
be indiscreet. Now the anxious urgings
about secrecy paid off. German Intelligence reports examined after the
war revealed that not a single word
about the coming attack was spoken
by any of the five officers or 231 other
ranks who were captured.

91

8th August – zero hour

Zero hour on 8th August was 4.20am. Behind the lines, Haig woke early, and noted in his diary:

'Glass steady. Fine night and morning – a slight mist in the valley. An autumn feel in the morning air . . . '

For Fourth Army, lying out under the stars, it had been a reasonably quiet night, enlivened only by a short German bombardment near Villers-Bretonneux, after an alert German post had reported 'Tommy in fighting kit lying out in front of the German positions'. There was no general German alarm, however, and the British troops remained still, accepting the casualties, waiting.

The attack front stretched from the River Ancre in the north down to Moreuil in the south – a twenty-mile length of line of which Fourth Army was responsible for thirteen miles, and Debeney for seven. On the Ancre, the British III Corps would provide the northern flank for the attack, while the main punch, in the centre, would be delivered by the Australian and Canadian Corps. The southern flank belonged to the XXXI Corps of Debeney's French First Army. On the staff maps, the successive objectives were marked in coloured lines: the Green Line, nearly four miles on from the start; the Red Line, three more miles on in the centre, though not so far on the flanks; and the Blue Line, which marked a total advance of around seven miles from the jumping-off positions. Beyond the Blue Line was the cratered moon-landscape of the Somme, taken by the Germans in the spring.

Just before Zero, the tanks moved up from their waiting positions a couple of miles back from the line. Mechanical reliability was much improved and of the 420 tanks available – 324 heavies and 96 Whippets – only five were not ready for action. Thirteen supply tanks, however, had been burned out in a conflagration after an unlucky shell had plunged into the orchard where they had been hidden near Villers-Bretonneux. The blaze had attracted a considerable German bombardment of the area, but there was still no German apprehension, at higher command levels, of a British tank attack.

Silence had been the watchword in Fourth Army as men, horses and machines moved up. Amiens, of course had been emptied of civilians for some time, and only soldiers moved through its darkened streets. Driving into the city not long before Zero, an observer noted that 'we began to pass British cavalry – their horses lined at the rightside of the road, heads towards us, evidently waiting to move off. As we got into Amiens itself (it now being practically dark) we found this cavalry moving quietly through the streets. It was wonderfully arranged. The paved streets were empty except for the cavalry column, and so they were able to move two columns abreast . . . The British cavalry columns were paired off exactly as in a review, always precisely abreast. If there was a cart beside us, then there was a cart beside it, paired off almost wheel for wheel – two carts, two wagons, twenty pairs of wagons, twenty pairs of guns, two streams of horsemen – all streaming the same way on the pale clean cobblestones through the dark winding streets. Before we reached the centre of the city they moved off by some avoiding road round the boulevards to the south . . . ' In such good order, and with high hopes, the British cavalry rode to the battle which would finally demonstrate, to those who had eyes to see, that there was no longer a place for them in full-scale modern war.

An hour before Zero, a white mist began to rise from the warm damp ground. By 3.40am it was so thick that there were fears that the aircraft meant to drown the noise of the tanks would not be able to take off, but these apprehensions proved groundless. Nevertheless, the mist, as at Hamel, was going to pose problems for both men and machines.

Above: 8th August 1918. German prisoners bring in a wounded officer.
Below: A direct hit by shellfire

For some little time before 4.20 there had been a steady bickering of gunfire on the III Corps front, where the angry aftermath of the Württembergers' raid was still occupying the attention of both British and Germans. This distant rumble was obliterated at the moment of Zero, when the 2,000 guns on Rawlinson's front, plus those of Debeney to the south, opened fire in a single titanic clap of sound. With sporadic, hoarse cheers at intervals along the line, the Australians and Canadians, cigarettes lit, rifles slung, moved out into the open.

At once, the planned formations broke up in the mist. It had been intended to operate in three waves – a thin line of scouts, with the job of indicating German positions to the tanks, then the tanks themselves, and last, about 150 yards back, the main body of the infantry, moving by sections in single-file columns. As at Hamel, however, the dust and pulverised soil kicked up by the supporting artillery fire combined with the mist to make it impossible to see for more than a few yards. The creeping barrage had been arranged to fall 200 yards ahead of the infantry at Zero, and then to pause for three minutes while the infantry closed up. It would then be lifted 100 yards every two minutes for the next 200 yards, after which it would lift 100 yards every three minutes until it had moved 1,000 yards from the point at which it had opened at Zero. This required a very exact rate of infantry advance, and a precise knowledge by infantry officers and NCOs of where they were at any given moment.

In the event, the advancing Australians found that the sound of the barrage itself was the only way of knowing just how far they had advanced in the first few minutes: some of them, pressing on too far in the dust-laden fog, entered the fringe of the barrage and died under a rain of their own shells. The fine quality of Australian junior officers and NCOs prevented what could have been a dangerous milling of troops in front of enemy positions. Forming themselves into improvised, shadowy battle groups, they pressed on into the fog which hung over the German line, while from time to time they entered trenches containing small German machine gun posts, whose occupants were peering anxiously out into the murk. As a rule, these German outposts surrendered hastily, but occasionally a braver man would hammer away with his Maxim until a bomb or a rifle shot from the flank ended his life.

The mist was not entirely to the Australians' disadvantage. In some cases, forward German units of considerable size were enveloped and overwhelmed before they fully realised what was happening. The 18th German Infantry Regiment of the 41st Division, which met the assault of the 7th Australian Brigade, suddenly found itself being attacked from the rear. Of the 715 officers and men in its two forward battalions, only 8 officers and 50 men escaped. One of the battalion headquarters, containing piles of documents, was captured, and an orderly on horseback galloped back to the Australian brigadier with the Intelligence 'loot'.

In the murk, many of the tanks floundered at first, losing their broad white guiding tapes in the first few yards, and with only the flash of German guns to show them where the enemy lay. However, towards 5.30, the mist began to lift in the warmth of the rising August sun, and the big Mark Vs at last began to play their full part. The 2nd and 3rd Australian Divisions were now closing with the Green Line on their sector. The tanks moved up beside and ahead of the infantry, making straight for the places where opposition was strongest, and causing terror and confusion in the German line.

'Everything', says a German battalion account, 'was affected by the fearful impression that the fire-vomiting iron dragons had made on artillery and infantry. A true tank-panic had seized on everything and where any dark shapes moved, men saw the black monster. "Everything is lost" was the cry that met the incoming battalions . . .'

North of Warfusee, Australian infantry of the 5th Brigade, supported by tanks, came upon the almost unprecedented sight of a German field battery waiting to be captured, its gunners seated passively on the trails. In Warfusee itself a tank led a small party of infantry to seize an abandoned battery of 4.2-inch guns. Although hit twice by a more determined battery about 800 yards away, it succeeded in towing one trophy back to the Australian positions. From time to time, in front of the Green Line, the tanks found a new obstacle – groups of contact mines which were capable of blowing off a track. These were roughly the size of cans of kerosene, and were buried in groups of six, with just the top couple of inches above the ground.

It was now around 7am, and the Australians, almost everywhere, were on the Green Line, their first objective. The advance had been astonishingly bloodless for Monash's troops: fewer than a thousand had been killed or wounded, and, according to the Official History, hardly a German shell had fallen since 5.40am. The next two Australian divisions, the 4th and the 5th, also supported by tanks, began to pass through to begin the jump-off to the Red Line. Under the sun, the mist rolled away across the Somme valley, and there was no more than a haze on the slopes north of the river. For those who had time to watch, it was an astonishing sight – a sight, said one observer, 'that the French and the British – and among them the Australians – had steadily looked for through four years of unbelievable trial . . .'

Where the fringe of the German line had run, the whole apparatus of the

Captured German machine gun near Sailly-Laurette, 8th August 1918

Fourth Army offensive was rolling forward as though nothing would ever stop it. All across the top of the Villers-Bretonneux plateau, Australian infantry were digging in. Down below them rumbled forward lines of Mark V tanks, painted with the colours of their accompanying infantry, or festooned with plaques showing the arms of the Australian battalions. Farther back still, and more colourful, the horsed field artillery moved up, and behind them lines of ammunition wagons, water-wagons, and other stores. Finally, observing all, waiting, was the cavalry – the whole of the 1st Brigade, ready to exploit, with the lean shapes of 100 Whippets beside them. Practically all was moving east. Only the growing lines of sullen prisoners, and a few limping Mark Vs, filtered slowly back to the former Australian lines. On both German and Allied sides of the line, there began to be a growing sense that something of very great importance had happened in the past four hours.

Progress by Sir Arthur Currie's Canadians on the right had also been very satisfactory. Its leading brigades, hampered by the mist at the start, had reached the Green Line by 7.45am. One battalion, the 16th Canadian Scottish, mounted a piper on a Mark V to guide its companies forward. He was killed, still playing, a few minutes later. Three of the Canadian divisions were in the line – the 2nd, 1st and 3rd, from left to right – with the 4th a mile or so in reserve. The 3rd Canadian Division had a difficult time at first, as the bad visibility seriously hampered the tanks, so that in some cases they were able to give little more than moral support. The division was also badly affected by the decision that the French troops on its immediate right should not move forward at Zero: in fact, although Debeney's barrage started on time, his infantry paused for about three quarters of an hour before beginning the as-

Canadian infantry, with British tank support, tackle a machine gun nest

German 15cm howitzer

sault. The resultant difficulties on the 3rd Division's right flank are not hard to imagine. The Canadians had already experienced considerable liaison difficulties with the local French command. A binational liaison force had been established to link the two forces, consisting of a section of the 94th Regiment of the French 42nd Division, with a machine gun, and a platoon of the 43rd Canadian Battalion, all commanded by a French officer. The French division had a British liaison officer, and the 3rd Canadian Division a French one. However, this proved to be inadequate, and when Deville, the French divisional comder, called on Lipsett, his Canadian opposite number, a day or two before the attack, there had been plenty of goodwill but little mutual comprehension. Deville could not speak English and Lipsett could not speak French. Even worse, Lipsett's GSO 1, his chief staff officer, spoke only a few

words of French. It was a strangely inadequate basis on which to start a great joint undertaking.

However, in spite of the difficulties, the Canadians attacked gallantly and with a will, and soon began to make good progress, though not without galling initial losses. The 9th Brigade of the 3rd Division, for instance, had a stiff fight in front of Hamon Wood, where the tanks were unable to give proper support. The leading company of its 116th Battalion lost all its officers and sixty men in the first few minutes, but held its own position and gave covering fire while the other three companies of the battalion outflanked and finally cleared the wood.

Less than a mile to the east, a single tank of A Company of the 5th Tank Battalion showed what could be done when tanks managed to overcome their difficulties and move up with the infantry. This machine spotted a German howitzer battery firing from sunken ground not far from Hamon Wood, but had been unable to get to grips with it because of the stout trees which intervened. Nevertheless, it had managed to waddle round the wood to the north and finally found a gap in the flank, from which it suddenly emerged to cover the terrified gun crew with its machine guns, until the Canadian infantry moved up through the trees and captured them. At this point, too, the mist was clearing, and German lines and their supply roads were systematically harassed by streams of British fighters and bombers in attacks from low level.

In the Canadian centre, the 1st Division was supported by B and C companies of the 4th Tank Battalion. These tanks found better going, and they swiftly demoralised the German infantry as, with clanking metal and stammering machine guns, they loomed out of the mist. Parties of Germans fled or surrendered only half-dressed: one regimental commander and all his staff were captured in a quarry. Where it remained steady, however, German artillery took steady toll of the tanks, and of the twenty-one machines which began the attack only twelve reached the Green Line with the infantry a little after 8am. By now the 2nd Division, on the left, had also reached this first objective. The Canadian Corps commander, Sir Arthur Currie, had cause for considerable satisfaction.

The drama of the Australian and Canadian operations in the centre of the Fourth Army line was, however, not the whole story. What was happening on the left and right wings of the advance was also vital for the long day ahead. In the south, on the extreme right, Debeney – as we have seen – had paused according to plan before ordering his infantry out into the attack at 5.5am. Debeney's pause, significantly enough, had been dictated by his lack of heavy tank support, since he had only two battalions of the light Renaults in an exploiting role. The French attacked with two divi-

General Sir Arthur Currie, commander of the Canadian Corps

sions on a two-mile front towards Moreuil, and their early progress was not without difficulties of morale. During the day, Haig drove to French First Army headquarters at Conty to speak to Debeney, recording later that he found him 'much distressed and almost in tears because three battalions of his Colonial infantry had bolted before a German machine gun . . .'

However, Debeney's sudden extension of the battle did much to disconcert the Germans facing Fourth Army's right flank. Moreuil soon fell to the French XXXI Corps, and the Avre was crossed, after a brisk battle, late in the morning. The French casualties for the day reached 3,500, but in prisoners alone they accounted for 5,000 Germans and 161 guns.

It was in the north, where the British III Corps was attacking on the Ancre, that the most ominous signs for the future development of the battle began to be noted. The role of III Corps had been to secure the Amiens outer defences between the Somme and the Ancre, as a flank to the main Australian-Canadian attack in the centre. The battleground for this operation was much more difficult than that farther south, and the tank support available for the British divisions was scanty, amounting to only twenty-two tanks of the 10th Tank Battalion, and twelve supply tanks. Over the seamed, ravine-strewn ground, the British troops, with Bell's American 33rd Division in reserve, managed to reach parts of the Green Line – the first objective – by 8am, but thereafter progress was slow and hesitant.

This meant that the vital Chipilly spur beside the River Somme was not captured in time to protect the Australian left flank when, in the next phase, Monash's corps moved forward.

A British supply tank rolls forward

As we shall see, the Australians soon began to lose many men in galling fire from this tenaciously-held German position, and the 'diggers' were to have unpleasant things to say about the soldierly qualities of III Corps before the day was out.

The difficulties of the ground and the lack of tanks, though they certainly contributed to the frustration of III Corps, are not sufficient entirely to explain it. There were two further reasons: one purely military, and one of morale. Ironically enough, the military one had been provided by the Australians themselves. Their ill-judged raid of 29th July, just before they handed over the sector to III Corps, had been followed, as we have seen, by the German reprisal raid of 6th August – only two days before the Fourth Army attack. This had hit the 18th British Division badly, and had completely upset the corps plan. Possibly more important, however, was the factor of morale. Neither the Australian nor the Canadian contingents had experienced the rough handling suffered by the British during Ludendorff's spring offensive. All four divisions of III Corps – the 58th, 18th, 12th and 47th – had been either in the line or in immediate reserve for the whole of 1918. The 58th alone had lost 3,530 officers and men at Villers-Bretonneux in April. Many of the division's most experienced and battle-hardened officers and NCOs were already in their graves, and young draftees sent out from Britain had scarcely had time to get their boots muddy. In the words of the Official History, 'these convalescent divisions had not entered with great enthusiasm on the hard task of preparing a field of battle, in the hours of darkness, and in bad weather . . .' As the morning advanced, there would be plenty of courage and determination from III Corps, but there would also be evidence that the British task had been underestimated in relation to the resources, human and material, available for its completion.

8th August – onward, flesh and metal

In spite of the difficulties on the left flank, however, a gap almost twelve miles long had been torn in the German defences opposite the Fourth Army centre. The sweep forward of the Australian and Canadian infantry, supported by their British tanks, was now vigorously pressed forward. The Canadians had seized part of the second objective, the Red Line, by 11am, and the Australians, where they were not inhibited on the left by German retention of the Chipilly spur, were on a portion of it by 9.30am and much of the rest an hour later. By half past one in the afternoon, the greater portion of the third objective, the Blue Line, was in Australian and Canadian hands.

The situation, by the standards of previous campaigns, was ripe for decisive exploitation. Marwitz had suffered a considerable disaster. Fourth Army had moved forward seven miles in nine hours. The Germans had lost 26,000 men in dead, wounded, and captured, and also 400 guns. It was Hamel multiplied by ten. Yet the following hours were to prove that the means for exploitation did not yet exist, that the cavalry was still the only available means, and that the cavalry was doomed. First, however, there were to be gleams of mechanised hope as well as clouds of frustration, and there would also be one or two moments of battle when the future of warfare could clearly be discerned.

The first of such moments was provided by the 17th Armoured Car Battalion. The sixteen cars of this unit – each with two turrets containing a machine gun – were put through the 4th Australian Division at the moment that the Australian infantry were closing with the Red Line objective. Passing unscathed through the fringe of the British support barrage, they found themselves on good roads, moving into heavy German traffic just behind the front. Turning into the Morecourt valley, they at once opened fire on the German infantry assembly areas, causing fantastic confusion.

Moving east, they raked the supply dumps along the road, and disabled a train. A few minutes later, they split into two main sections – one moving south on Framerville, and the other north on Proyart. The Framerville section almost instantly began a spectacular action, finding a stream of transport wagons just outside the village, sending a hail of bullets into the lines of horses. In a few moments the roads were covered with dying men and animals, while the plunging rearing survivors overturned their wagons, and crashed into each other. Moving quickly into the southern end of the village, this handful of cars now began to cut down astonished Germans who ran to the doors of the houses to see what was going on. Four staff officers on horseback were killed by a single burst. The commander of one car dismounted at the door of a large, important-looking house, and entered it, revolver in hand. He found the rooms empty of men but full of documents, some of them hurriedly torn up by the fleeing German staff. All he could find was stuffed into sandbags and loaded into the car. He then nailed a small Australian flag above the door and drove away. Inside one of the sandbags, eagerly examined a little later by Intelligence officers, was a plan of part of the Hindenburg Line. This officer's report, sent by pigeon, was a model of satisfied brevity:

'Enemy infantry surrendering very freely. Have sent scores back and killed scores, others running away. Enemy artillery nil. Have toured round Framerville and upset all their transport, etc. Australian flag hoisted at 11.15 on German Corps HQ . . .'

The section of cars which probed into Proyart found an even more vulnerable target. The village was the advanced headquarters of the German LI Corps, and its staff were just sitting down to a meal. The cars poured fire through the windows of the dining hall, missing the corps commander, who had left in his car about thirty minutes before. Passing on through the Ger-

Above: German transport at Franerville after a British armoured car raid
Below: A carrier pigeon leaves its tank

Still hoping to exploit a breakthrough, British cavalry move up on Le Quesnel, 9th August 1918

man rear areas, the cars caused yet more havoc and confusion, and eventually returned inside the Australian lines. Nine cars had been damaged, though all were repairable. In such a way did a handful of machines, with daring crews, create chaos for the withdrawal of an entire German corps, and strike a telling blow against German morale.

Meanwhile, for the cavalry, it was a more depressing story. Some useful work was, of course, done: squadrons galloped where they could to pick up German prisoners and guns – often those who had surrendered earlier to the tanks. But the attempts to combine Whippets and cavalry as a destructive force were a failure, as Fuller had foreseen. The Whippet belied its name. Capable of about 9mph on the road, it could do only about 4mph over open country. The result was predic-table: while advancing, the Whippets could not keep up with the cavalry and as soon as they came under fire the flesh and blood of the cavalry could no longer stay with the steel of the Whippets. No proper thinking had been done about Whippet-cavalry co operation, and this led, on the evening of 8th August, to the absurd outcome that when, before dusk, the cavalry retired to water their horses, the Whippets retired with them.

Occasionally, however, there was a glitter of the old cavalry glory, as when the 15th Hussars, attacking at Guillacourt on the left of the Canadian line, galloped to battle in successive waves of steel-helmeted horsemen sabres drawn, rifles in their leather buckets, and seized trenches a mile in front of the infantry, holding them dismounted, by rifle fire. In truth there was no want of courage in the British cavalry. Throughout the long day, the battlefield was dotted with fallen, writhing men and horses who had died because the cavalry was living n the past. The facts were now there or all to see. The machine gun had nded the role of the cavalry, and orsemen could not attack entrenchnents which were defended by machne guns and accurate riflemen. The avalryman had one lethal disadvanage on the battlefield of modern war. Ie could not lie down and take cover. Iothing could outweigh this crippling nandicap.

The Royal Horse Artillery also suffered from the vulnerability of the horse, and during the day batteries, ager to get into action as soon as possible, were often held back too long y anxious brigade and divisional ommanders who preferred to rely on onventional field artillery, and save he mobile arm for some hypothetical xtension of the battle. The remaining hreds of elegance, in fact, were going ut of warfare for the last time, but here were one or two memorable noments. An Australian observer,

sitting in the steaming meadows of the Somme valley as the sun dispersed the mist, saw a sight that remained with him long after the war:

'Past us . . . trooped a procession of Royal Horse Artillery behind the wood. They were led by a young officer, riding round-backed, in the most immaculate dress. He carried a riding switch like a field-marshal's baton in his right hand. His helmet was covered with some terracotta stuff which looked like chamois leather; and he wore chamois leather gloves unbuttoned at the wrist, going into action as he would go off to Rotten Row . . . Behind rode his trumpeter, and, farther behind, the battery, every man's helmet the same terracotta colour and tilted at the same angle, the horses walking easily, tossing their chestnut manes. It was A Battery of the Royal Horse

Australian infantry come out of the line after several days hard fighting

Guns of the Royal Horse Artillery at the gallop

Artillery, the famous Chestnut Troop, going forward...'

The Battle of Amiens, however, was not a field where such *panache* could find its proper reward. Sitting in a tree at the side of the valley, the same elegant young officer found that the day was to be one of frustration, recording himself later:

'No favourable targets as the Hun infantry were all surrendering ... I saw a Hun gun firing in the open and cantered back for a gun to take it on, but found an Australian battery was doing so; in fact they were ahead of us all day in that respect, having started by attaching one section to each attacking battalion...'

Paradoxically, there actually was one real cavalry moment on 8th August, and it came, not from men on horseback, but from men in a machine – from the crew of a single Whippet tank of B Company of the 6th Tank Battalion. The tank, 'Musical Box', was commanded by Lieutenant C B Arnold, and it was to fight what is arguably the greatest single-tank action in the history of war.

Arnold and his crew, Gunner C Ribbans and Driver W J Carney, left their lying-up point at zero hour and moved across country with the rest of the company to the railway at Villers-Bretonneux, which they crossed, and later passed through the Australian infantry of the 2nd Division. He then turned along the side of the railway, and found himself in the lead and alone, the other tanks of his section having become ditched in the difficult ground. He came under very heavy shellfire, and watched as two Mark Vs, operating on his right, went up in flames. He at once engaged the German battery which had hit the Mark Vs, moving diagonally across the German guns, while they frantically fired eight rounds at him without getting a direct hit. Running along a belt of trees at the side of the road, he finally emerged at the rear of the battery. In the next few moments, he and Gunner Ribbans shot down the entire German gun crew, numbering about thirty men. Arnold's basic task, of course, was to cooperate with the cavalry, and he began a momentous hour by doing just this. His own words, written in January 1919, describe best what happened:

'I cruised forward, making a detour to the left, and shot a number of the enemy who appeared to be demoralised and were moving about the country in all directions ... Then moved off again, passing through two cavalry patrols of about twelve men each. The first patrol was receiving casualties from a party of enemy in a field of corn. I dealt with this, killing three or four, the remainder escaping out of sight into the corn. Proceeding further east, I saw the second patrol pursuing six enemy. The leading horse was so tired that he was not gaining appreciably on the rearmost Hun. Some of the leading fugitives turned about and fired at the cavalryman when his sword was stretched out and practically touching the back of the last Hun. Horse and rider were brought down on the left of the road. The remainder of the cavalrymen deployed to the right, coming in close under the railway embankment, where they dismounted and came under fire from the enemy, who had now taken up a position on the railway bridge, and were firing over the parapet, inflicting one or two casualties. I ran the machine up until we had a clear view of the bridge, and killed four of the enemy with one long burst, the other two running across the bridge and so down the opposite slope out of sight...'

Arnold now continued to move east, beside the railway, until Musical Box entered a small valley between Bayonvillers and Harbonnieres. The valley was lined with German hutments, and full of troops who were packing their kits. Arnold at once opened fire and cleared the valley. A few minutes later Ribbans dismounted and counted about sixty dead and wounded Germans. His adventure, however, was by no means over. His account continues:

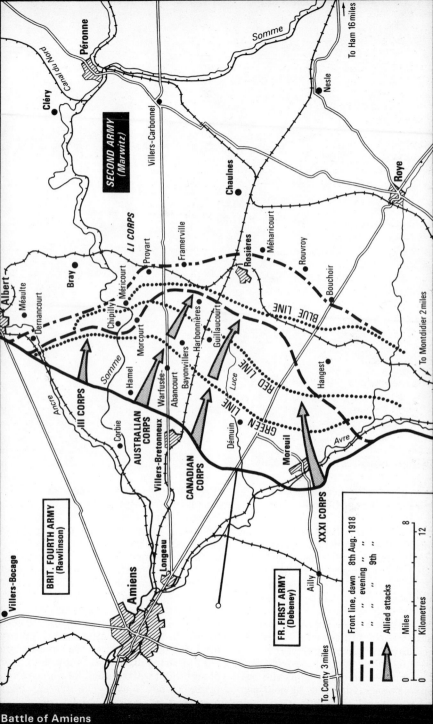

Battle of Amiens

German gun and limber caught by British shellfire near Chapilly

'I turned left from the railways and cruised across country, as lines of enemy infantry could be seen retiring. We fired at these many times at ranges of 200 yards to 600 yards. These targets were fleeting, owing to the enemy getting down into the corn when fired upon. In spite of this, many casualties must have been inflicted, as we cruised up and down for at least an hour . . .'

By this time, the crew of Musical Box were in some distress, as the bullet splash on the hull and the heat produced by several hours of action made it necessary for them to breathe through the mouthpieces of their standard box respirators, though they did not put on the masks. However, they went on with this strange, lonely battle, and at two o'clock in the afternoon they ran into the transport of two German regiments of the 225th Division, together with its instructional school. Arnold saw it as:

'. . . great. quantities of motor and horse transport moving in all directions. On the top of another bridge to my left I could see the cover of a lorry coming in my direction. I moved up out of sight and waited until he topped the bridge, when I shot the driver. The lorry ran into a right-hand ditch . . .

'I could see a long line of men retir-

ing on both sides of the railway and fired at these at ranges of 400 to 500 yards, inflicting heavy casualties. I passed through these and also accounted for one horse and the driver of a two-horse canvas covered wagon on the far side of the railway. We now crossed a small road which crossed the main railway and close to it. Gunner Ribbans (right hand gun) here had a view of the south side of the railway, and fired continuously into motor and horse transport moving on three roads. . . . I fired many bursts at 600 to 800 yards at transport blocking roads to my left, causing great confusion . . .'

A few moments later, Musical Box, its gun ports shot away, was ablaze.

Its three-man crew baled out, rolling over and over on the ground to extinguish their burning uniforms. During this activity Driver Carney was shot in the stomach and killed. Arnold and Ribbans, after being kicked and beaten up with rifle butts, and slapped by a German officer, were taken prisoner. The burned-out wreck of Musical Box, the little Whippet tank which had single-handed brought to battle a great portion of the rear of the German Second Army, was later found by advancing British troops close to the railway on the eastern side of the Harbonnieres-Rosieres road.

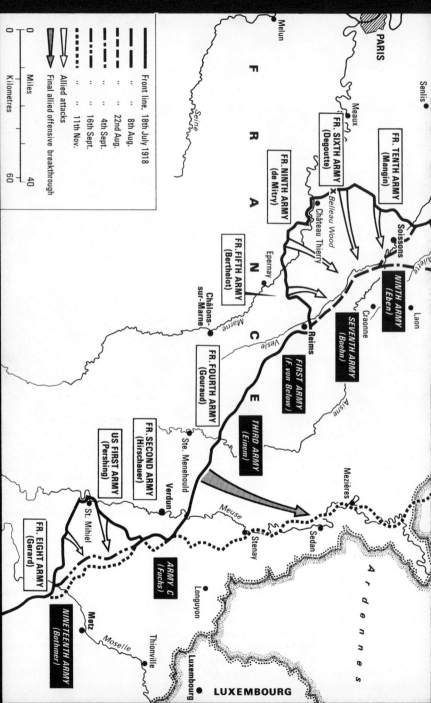

Slowing down

It had been an amazing day. The German front had splintered and buckled along fifteen miles of its length. Nearly 700 German officers and about 27,000 men had been killed, seriously wounded, or taken prisoner, and 400 guns had been lost. 'We have practically eaten up seven Prussian divisions', Rawlinson wrote exultantly in his diary the following day. Winston Churchill, driving on the same day along the road which ran east from Amiens to Vermand, also sensed the nature of the blow which the German armies had sustained:

'Off we went . . . through deserted, battered, ghostly Amiens; through Villers-Bretonneux, a heap of smouldering wreckage, threading our way through the intervals of an endless convoy which moved slowly from one shell-hammered point to another . . . The German dead lay everywhere, but scattered in twos and threes and half-dozens over a very wide area. Rigid in their machine gun nests, white flaccid corpses, lay those faithful legionaries of the Kaiser who had tried to stem the rout of six battle-worthy German divisions. A British war balloon overhead burst into a sheet of fire, from which tiny black figures fell in parachutes. Cavalry cantered as gaily over the reconquered territory as if they themselves were the cause of victory. By a small wood seven or eight tanks with scattered German dead around them lay where a concealed battery had pierced them, twisted and scorched by fierce petrol fires in which they had perished. "Crews nearly all burned to death," said the officer of the burying party. "Those still alive are the worst off . . ."'

And yet, on 9th August, there were already ominous signs for the Allies that exploitation of the previous day's victory in a purely military sense might be much more difficult than at first appeared. The attack instrument itself – the British tank force – had been badly blunted. Of the 415 tanks which had actually entered the battle, only 145 were available for 9th August.

The others were either knocked out by enemy guns, still ditched, or mechanically unserviceable. The other instrument for the hoped-for decision, the cavalry, had already lost about 1,000 horses, and was to lose nearly as many more in the next few days.

More important still, there could now be no Monash-type clockwork battle. The plans for exploitation were imprecise, possibly because the battle had now reached the tangled mass of rusting wire and battered trenches which formed the old Somme battlefield. This was not a battleground over which it was possible to plan a meticulous, exactly-timed operation. Rawlinson himself clearly recognised this, recording that 'the country over which we shall be working is seamed with old trenches which will be full of machine gun nests, so I fear we shall have a high casualty list . . .'

The concentrated blow of Fourth Army upon a comparatively narrow front, which had been an important element in its success when supported by 415 tanks on 8th August, was inevitably less effective when supported by 145 tanks on the following day. The attack had been frontal: indeed, it could not be anything else. Its decisive element had been surprise, which had achieved the swift overrunning of the outer ring of German divisions. However, as with any frontal attack, its impetus slowed as it pushed farther and farther into the mass of rapidly-assembled German reserves. Thus 9th August was a day of hard but patchy fighting, resulting in some territorial gains, but in nothing which at any point looked decisive even in a local sense. The crowded roads in the newly-captured areas made communications difficult: brigades and divisions attacked at varying times and in a disjointed way: the German gunners began to find that when the tanks loomed up on a clear day instead of out of the frightening mist, they were not difficult to knock out, provided a cool head was kept. Meanwhile, Ludendorff, hastily opposing some suggestions of a

Above: A tank comes to pull out another, one track of which has slipped over the edge of a flooded road. *Below:* German Maxim gun team in prone position

**Experimental Mark V Star tank using a
trench crossing 'bridge'**

withdrawal to the Hindenburg Line,
began to plug the German Second
Army gap with nine divisions. Three
of these arrived on the evening of 8th
August from Rupprecht's reserves,
while six more were approximately in
position by the afternoon of the next
day. In view of all this, Rawlinson
could express a qualified satisfaction
in the results of the day's fighting for
his Fourth Army, which gave him an
advance of nearly five miles in the
south, and ended with his troops holding a line Bouchoir-Rouvroy-Mehari-
court-Framerville-Mericourt-Derna-
ncourt.

The omens were becoming distinctly
less promising. Of the 145 tanks which
began the day, 78 were lost, leaving
only 67 for 10th August. The German
gunners were learning fast, and the
Australian 8th Brigade had watched in
consternation during the morning
when six Mark Vs supporting Australian infantry forward near Harbonnieres were knocked out in quick
succession by a single German gun
hidden in a farm shed. Unprotected by
tanks, the attacking battalion lost
twelve officers in the next few minutes. The Canadians, too, were finding
that tank warfare was not a one-way
business. The 16th Canadian Scottish
passed a sad scene at Rouvroy, and the
battalion account recorded later that
'the men knew what had happened to
the attack of the morning. The dere-
lict tanks, demolished by direct hits,
the inside of them like charnel houses,
the dead men and dead horses scattered everywhere around, told very
surely of its location and fate . . .'

There had also been difficulties with
one new type of tank from which much
had been hoped. This was the Mark V
Star, a lengthened version of the Mark
V, which had greatly improved trench
crossing ability, and was also capable
of lifting about twenty men. The in-

Death of a tank soldier

terior of the tank, however, became so hot and fume-laden that infantry passengers arrived vomiting and even delirious at the delivery points. One Australian account describes how in one tank 'everyone had collapsed. None had the strength to push open the doors. All were carried or helped to sunken ground near by where they lay for over an hour before any could move himself . . .' The mobile, armoured infantry carrier was still some years away.

Meanwhile, the British III Corps, reinforced by a three-battalion regiment of Americans – the 131st – had redeemed itself during the morning with a determined attack on the Chipilly spur. Both British and Americans suffered heavily from German machine gun fire as they made this arduous assault – the Americans especially since they had to rush the last mile forward to reach the German positions. Their dash and style won the admiration of the British command, and the Fourth

Army account of the battle says that they swept everything before them '. . . it was due to them that the objective was so quickly and rapidly gained . . .' Before the day ended, the whole of the Chipilly spur was in British and American hands.

Just as 9th August had been less productive than 8th August, so 10th August was less productive than 9th August. The tank situation was now parlous, with only sixty-seven fit for battle. The attacking corps were weary and short of sleep, and enemy resistance was steadily stiffening as Ludendorff and the German command brought their reserve divisions into play. Most weary of all were the tank crews of the surviving machines. The effects on them of such a long battle had been under-estimated. In a latter analysis of the fighting, Fuller wrote that 'on account of the lack of reserves it was found impossible to maintain a sound tactical organisation after the first day. With unlimited or distant objectives it is essential, if fighting is to be effective, to keep a strong reserve in hand, so that a continuous *roulement* of units may be kept up . . . Infantry commanders do not yet appreciate the exhaustive nature of tank fighting . . . The taxi-cab system of using tanks, that is, of whistling them up whenever required, is still constantly used – and it is absolutely wrong . . . The duty of the tanks is to silence the enemy's machine guns so that the infantry may continue their advance. Equally it is the duty of the infantry to silence the enemy's guns so that the tanks may not be knocked out. This form of cooperation has not yet been cultivated . . .'

The offensive of the Fourth Army was petering out, and Rawlinson, worrying about another Cambrai in which all would suddenly turn to dust and ashes, knew it. On 11th August, with only thirty-eight tanks left, it was becoming imperative to close the battle down. This had already been

Stuck fast near Chapilly

under consideration by Haig since the previous day, and it was to cause a sharp division of opinion in the Allied command. Rawlinson and Haig were in favour of ending the battle, and replacing it with new operations by the armies on the flanks, but the *generalissimo*, Foch, wished to press on with the frontal assault.

Foch had visited Haig at Wiry on 10th August, taking with him a directive which ordered Fourth Army to continue east towards Ham, with the intention of seizing bridgeheads over the Somme below the town. Meanwhile, the French First and Third Armies would extend the battle to the right, clearing the whole of the Mondidier area. Haig was opposed to this continuation of the frontal attack. He wanted to use the British Third Army east of Amiens to produce a new threat on the flank of the present battle. Foch was willing to agree to this, but only if the operation was carried out in conjunction with a renewed effort by Rawlinson and Debeney in the centre. He believed that the German divisions were now so demoralised as to offer the chance of a decisive stroke.

At first, Haig gave way. The GHQ operation order of 10th August insisted that 'the offensive operations of the French First Army and the British Fourth Army will be continued with a view to securing the general line Guiscard-Ham-Peronne and gaining the crossings of the River Somme ...'

Then, on the same afternoon, Haig went to the Canadian Corps headquarters at Demuin, and met both Rawlinson and Currie. Rawlinson was strongly against pushing his weary army any further forward. Haig told him stiffly that the order came from Marshal Foch. It is some indication of the nervous strain of battle upon even so imperturbable figure as Rawlinson that he rounded sharply upon Haig, asking truculently: 'Are you commanding the British army or is Marechal Foch?' It was a surprising liberty to take with a Commander-in-Chief and no doubt it both angered and disturbed Haig. But it had its intended effect, after it became clear that the fighting of 11th August was even less effective than that of 10th August. With Haig's approval, Rawlinson stopped the immediate continuation of the offensive, recording later: 'I have stopped the attack, and told the corps to rest and reorganise. We shall renew the attack on the 15th, deliberately, with as many tanks as we can collect ...'

By 14th August, it was becoming obvious that an assault on the reinforced German defences on the Somme would be a grievously costly affair. Fortunately for the lives of thousands of British, Empire and French soldiers, Rawlinson was equal to the occasion. He was no blind obeyer of orders. His diary entry for that evening records what took place:

'I went over to DH at 10am with maps and photographs of the objectives for the attack which had been arranged for tomorrow. I pointed out to him that we were up against a

egular trench system with masses of uncut wire, and I considered that to take it on with our present resources in guns and tanks would be to risk heavy losses and possible failure.

suggested that it would be far better and cheaper to hold the enemy to his ground, on my front, by wire-cutting and bombardment until the Third Army is ready to put in a surprise attack, and then to press on simultaneously with that attack . . . I left him the maps and photographs to show to Foch . . . '

Haig was now becoming strongly of the opinion that Rawlinson was right and that Foch was wrong. He ordered Rawlinson to postpone his attack, and went to see Foch at Sarcus in the afternoon. Haig's own diary takes up the story:

'I had ordered the French First and British Fourth Armies to postpone their attacks, but to keep up pressure on that front so as to make the enemy expect an attack on this front, while I transferred my reserves to my Third

Troops bring back salvage from the battlefield to a regimental aid post on the III Corps front

Army (Byng) and also prepared to attack with the First Army (Horne) on the front Monchy-le-Preux – Miraumont. Foch now wanted to know what orders I had issued for attack? When I proposed to attack? Where, and with what troops?'

If Foch thought that such a brisk quiz would put effective pressure on the British commander, he had sadly mistaken his man. Haig's account continues:

'I told Foch of my instructions . . . and that Rawlinson would also co-operate with his left between the Somme and the Ancre when my Third Army had advanced . . . I spoke to Foch quite straightly and let him understand that *I was responsible to my government and fellow citizens for the handling of the British forces.* Foch's attitude at once changed, and he said that all he wanted was early informa-

A tank and stretcher bearers move
forward with the Allied advance

German ammunition shelters burn

tion of my intentions so that he might coordinate the operations of the other armies, and that he now thought I was quite correct in my decision not to attack the enemy in his prepared position. But notwithstanding what he said, Foch and all his staff had been most insistent for the last five days that I should press on along the south bank and capture the Somme bridges above Peronne, regardless of German opposition and British losses . . . '

As observed earlier, the British generals of the First World War have not, so far, had overmuch respect from history. Yet it would be difficult to over-estimate the importance of the firmness of Haig and Rawlinson in opposing the early wishes of Foch. If the attack had continued, it might well have driven into a bloody stalemate in the wilderness of the Somme battlefield. Ludendorff would have been vastly encouraged – and, as we shall see, that might have had a catastrophic effect upon the Allies' hopes for an early victory. Neither

Haig nor Rawlinson lacked military skills, but their greatest triumph was not of this nature. It was, indeed, a triumph of character.

In such a way the Battle of Amiens drew to its close, to be replaced, with Foch's belated approval, by an intelligent policy of raining repeated and successive blows on the German front farther to the north. Amiens, in the middle of August 1918, seemed to the Allied command to be a fine stroke, of limited but considerable scope, and a handsome portent for the future. Yet it was soon to be proved that 8th August was a much more important date than such an assessment would indicate; that it was, in fact, the date of the most decisive British battle since Waterloo. Fuller, shrewd and watchful with his tanks, had sensed the change that had come over the war on that misty morning. 'The Battle of Amiens,' he remarked, 'was the strategical end of the war . . . the rest was minor tactics . . . ' To see why this was so, we must move to the other side of the battle lines, where Lundendorff in his headquarters was reading the daily reports from his armies.

Defeat of a mind

The British military analyst Liddell Hart once laid down a dictum which said: 'It matters little what the situation actually was at any particular point or moment: all that matters is what the commander thought it was . . . ' The truth of this statement has never been more vividly shown than on 8th August 1918. It was this day which finally convinced Ludendorff that Germany could no longer hope to win the war. Yet the German armies had suffered no more than a sharp reverse; the German front had not been broken; and, as we have seen, within two or three days the Allied offensive would run out of steam. The real victory of Haig, Foch, Rawlinson and Debeney was over the mind of Ludendorff.

For weeks before 8th August, the conditions for toppling Ludendorff's mind had been there. They owed much to Mangin and his swarm of little Renault tanks on 18th July. At the end of June, asked by Germany's Foreign Minister, von Hintze, if he was 'confident of finally and decisively beating the enemy in the offensive now going on,' Ludendorff had said firmly: 'I can reply to that with a decided "yes".' It was the failure of this offensive, and the frightening, bewildering success of Mangin's armoured counterstroke, which brought Ludendorff to the edge of emotional collapse. The signs accumulated rapidly. Sitting at his desk, gloomily thumbing through his Moravian prayerbook and finding poor omens in the texts, quarrelling with his nominal chief, Hindenburg, at the headquarters dinner-table, taking an obsessive interest – strangely similar to the attitude of Adolf Hitler in his last days – in the minutiae of troop movements and the positioning even of individual battalions, Ludendorff began to cause concern to his staffs. One officer confided to his diary that his superiors were 'very much disturbed by the appearance and nervousness of His Excellency. It really does give the impression that he has lost all confidence. The army chiefs are suffering grievously as a result. Thus there are telephone conversations on the day's programme which last for one-and-a-half hours . . . ' That entry was made on 25th July.

Mangin's counterblow had forced Ludendorff to give up his cherished *Hagen* offensive against the British in Flanders. This change of plan seemed to leave him strategically paralysed: 'I had as yet no idea how, if at all, we should be able to recover the initiative . . . ', he wrote later. Hindenburg, too, shared the growing doubts, writing mournfully: 'How many hopes, cherished during the past two months, had collapsed. How many calculations had been scattered to the winds . . . '

Yet, between the end of July and the first week of August, the front had stabilised again and quietened down, and Ludendorff had so far recovered his equilibrium as to turn a stern eye upon the suspect *morale* of his own staff, asserting somewhat shrilly in a secret order that: 'Supreme Headquarters is free from despair. Sustained by what has previously been accomplished on the front and at home, it is ready stoutly to meet the challenges that are to come. No member of Supreme Headquarters may think and act in a manner other than this . . . ' To modern eyes, it is an order which, again, is strangely reminiscent of the directives issued from the *Führerbunker* in the spring of 1945.

It was into this scene of doubt and uncertainty that Rawlinson's attack burst on the morning of 8th August. The German view of what happened during the day is expressed in terms of despair in the official German monograph on the battle: 'As the sun set on 8th August on the battlefield the greatest defeat which the German Army had suffered since the beginning of the war was an accomplished fact. The position divisions between the Avre and the Somme, which had been struck by the enemy attack, were

Hindenburg (left) and Ludendorff

134

nearly completely annihilated . . . '

These terms seem somewhat grandiose for the loss of 27,000 men and a few hundred guns, especially since the gaps were being plugged by new troops from more than sixty divisions in reserve. Ludendorff's chief anxiety, in fact, was not the loss of men and material. He had sent a staff officer to the battlefield, and the report which followed had brought him fresh cause for alarm. He wrote later:

'I was told of deeds of glorious valour, but also of behaviour which, I openly confess, I should not have thought possible in the German army. Whole bodies of our men had surrendered to single troopers or isolated squadrons. Retiring troops, meeting a fresh division going into action, had shouted out things like "blackleg," and "you're prolonging the war" . . . Everything I feared . . . had here, in one place, become a reality. Our war machine was no longer efficient. Our fighting power had suffered . . . ' He summed it up in a famous, despairing phrase: 'August 8 was the Black Day of the German Army in the history of the war.'

This loss of confidence by Ludendorff in the instrument with which he had to work was fatal for him – as indeed it would have been for any commander. It is difficult at this reach of time to decide how far his anxieties about the spirit of his armies was justified. There had been factors adverse to German morale for some time, even before the spring offensive which had first renewed, then dashed, hopes of a German military victory. Troops returning from the Russian front had in some cases been infected by revolutionary fervour, and there had been mounting trouble and indiscipline along the railways and lines of communication to the front. The situation was in many ways aggravated by a peculiarly German characteristic – that of forming *élite* units, in this case by the

Germany's elite shock troops

137

American infantry advance towards the Argonne front in French-built tanks, September 1918

The Kaiser with Hindenburg and Ludendorff at Spa

grading of divisions as 'shock' divisions and 'trench' divisions. Many of the excellent 'shock' divisions had been badly cut about in the spring offensive, and it had been the poorer human material (in military terms) of the 'trench' divisions which had taken the brunt as Rawlinson's 400-odd tanks loomed out of the mist.

Something of the feelings of an intelligent and sensitive German soldier at this time can be gleaned from the diary of a German officer – the same man, in fact, who had suffered and shared the frustration of the abortive attack on 16th July, previously quoted. This entry was made on the evening of 12th August, two days after *der Schwartze Tag:*

'A lot of officers and men have just gone on leave and thought that they had earned it, and here we are being hauled out again to be shoved in just where it is warmest. I shudder to think of going through the Somm wilderness again for the fourth time It will be the same all over again, bu without any confidence. Our troop will be thinner and worse; for day the horses have not had a grain o oats; the men are being given barley bread which will not rise in the over and we have taken some knocks Against us we shall have thousands o tanks, tens of thousands of airmen hundreds of thousands of heart: young men, behind whom there wil be an American army which ma number a million . . . Last night dreamed I saw the Kaiser enterin what seemed to be the gateway of camp, bareheaded and on foot, force by his people to give himself up t their mercy. I don't know whether h ended on the scaffold, but I should no be surprised . . . '

The general background to the war indeed, was becoming more and mor discouraging to German soldiers The blockade meant that the letter received at the front from home often

mplained of increasing hardship
nd food shortages. There was a
gradually dawning realisation that
more and more American divisions
were arriving from a seemingly-
inexhaustible reservoir of manpower,
or out of reach across the Atlantic.
Yet soldiers on both sides of the
battle-lines were weary and sick of
war, and the German discontent had
ever yet approached the depths
suffered by the French army in the
mutinies which followed Nivelle's
disasters of 1917. Ludendorff's instrument might still be better than he
knew.

However, Ludendorff himself was
now moving in a shadowy world of
despair. His emotional crises mounted
in frequency and in intensity: his
moods varied between something
approaching panic and wild, irrational
optimism. His staff had already
secretly invited a psychiatrist to
come to Supreme Headquarters to
report on the mental condition of the
commander of the German armies.
The avalanche, however, had been
piling up for weeks and months of
struggle and trial, and the slide that
had begun on 8th August could not
be stopped. On 11th August, at Avesnes,
Ludendorff met the Kaiser, and laid
before him the full extent of his own
anxieties. He was in his most gloomy
mood, recording later:

'I had no hope of finding a strategic
expedient whereby to turn the situation to our advantage. Leadership
now assumed . . . the character of an
irresponsible game of chance, a thing
I have always considered fatal. The
fate of the German people was for me
too high a stake. The war must be
ended . . . '

Wilhelm II – who had already declined to accept Ludendorff's resig-
nation immediately after 8th August –
was surprisingly quick to accept his
view. He held out his hand to Ludendorff, and said firmly:

'I see we must balance the books,
we are at the limit of our powers. The
war must be brought to an end . . .

Accordingly I shall expect the commanders in chief at Spa in the course
of the next few days . . . '

The conference at Spa, which was
attended by Hertling (the German
Chancellor), von Hintze, Ludendorff,
Hindenburg and the Kaiser, was a
further revelation of how far Ludendorff's judgment had finally been unseated by the events of 8th August.
In a private talk with Hintze before
the main meeting, Ludendorff now
announced that he intended that 'by a
strategic defensive, we shall gradually
paralyse the enemy's spirit . . . '

Wilhelm II, however, after hearing
Ludendorff's new report of the military
situation, suggested that peace nego-
tiations should be opened through the
Queen of the Netherlands. Hintze
was basically in agreement, saying
that 'the political leaders accept the
verdict of the greatest general produced by the war. They infer that we
are unable to break the enemy by
military action, and that the policy to
be pursued must take into account
the military position . . . ' The hope
of victory was now abandoned, and
the search began to salve the best
possible solution from the wreck of
the hopes of the past four years. There
was one last flash of irrational defi-
ance from Ludendorff. The minutes of
the meeting, recording the slightly
more optimistic view of the situation
taken by the old Field-Marshal
Hindenburg, said: 'Hindenburg hopes
that in spite of everything he will be
able to stay on French soil and thus
eventually impose our will on the
enemy . . . ' Ludendorff read the minutes carefully, and in a sudden *volte-
face*, snatched a pen and struck out
the word 'hopes'. A soldier, he mut-
tered angrily, does not hope. In place
of the hated word, he substituted
'Hindenburg explains that he will
be able to . . . ' The words were brave,
but they were only words. Thousands
of men were yet to die, but Germany
had already lost the war.

The battle that never was

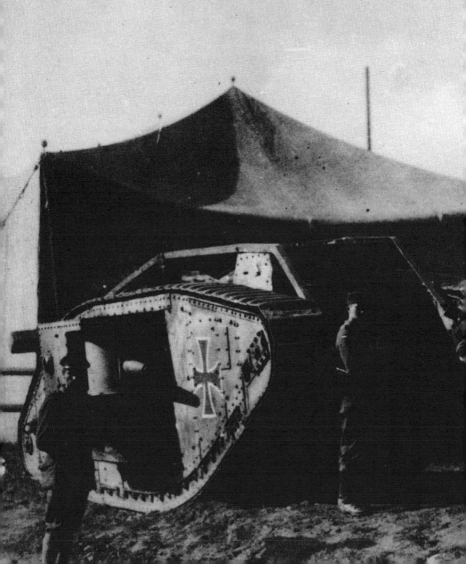

Thus 8th August was decisive, not on the ground, but in the German mind. There are too many imponderables in war for it ever to be classed as an exact science, and it will never be possible to quantify the extent to which the Allied success was due to the tank. Yet to study the available evidence is inevitably to come to the conclusion that there indeed was an armoured breakthrough in 1918, and that it was both material and psychological.

Exaggerated claims, of course, were made by tank propagandists on both sides. For the Germans, the Allied strength in tanks, and the German lack of them, sometimes became an excuse for military reverses which could not otherwise be conveniently explained. From 8th August onwards, German communiqués harped on the part played by tanks in every Allied success: 'masses of tanks' were often said to have been employed when examination of the Allied orders-of-battle show that only handfuls were used. Such an explanation was convenient to higher commands, but depressing to regimental soldiers, and the German press of 1918 shows increasing concern over the scanty numbers of German tanks.

Until the climactic events of 8th August the German attitude to tanks had been almost completely negative. Ludendorff had early given his view that 'as to the tanks, opinion was calm: they were not thought to be particularly dangerous . . . For ·defence against tanks, the field gun which penetrated them was sufficient; all we had to do was to turn it out in sufficient quantities . . . ' This view was to some extent reinforced, curiously enough, by the Battle of Cambrai. The comparative ease with which the German infantry and artillery won back their early losses helped to convince the German higher command that the tanks were a 'gimmick' weapon without much military future.

Nevertheless, opinion had been sufficiently impressed during 1916 and

1917 to begin active steps to develop though on a small scale, a German equivalent. In 1917 an order was placed for a newly-designed machine known as the A7V. This was a 30 tonner, with a crew of eighteen, and a 57mm gun, supported by six machine guns. Though it had many design defects, the A7V was not by any means an ineffective machine, and it is a telling indication of German half-heartedness about tanks to note that on no occasion during the war did the German tank force exceed 40 machines – about 15 A7Vs, and 25 captured British Mark IVs. The maximum number of tanks ever used by the Germans in a single operation was twenty. Ludendorff, like the Allies, was fighting a battle of attrition, but he was content to fight it with men and not with machines. He seemed never to grasp the enormous saving in manpower which the tank offered him, commenting ruefully after the war:

'Perhaps I ought to have made greater efforts, and possibly in tha

German wooden dummy tanks, built to deceive Allied airmen

case we should have had a few more tanks for the decision in 1918; but I do not know what other claims could have been set aside to enable them to have been built. We could not release any more workmen, and the people at home could not supply any more. *Had any been available, we should have wanted them as recruits . . .* '

Thus it was not until 8th August, when tanks were employed properly for the first time *en masse* in support of the infantry, that Ludendorff began to realise that the tank had revolutionised minor tactics, to the German army's disadvantage. German defence was based on the machine gun, which the German infantry used in the most effective and lethal manner. Suddenly the machine gun found itself invulnerably approached and the either knocked out or outflanked in the most disconcerting fashion. It was not that the tank was a great slaughterer of infantry. Unless its gunners were exceptionally good, their fire from the lurching, bucketing

hull was much too inaccurate for that. But the tank was a great outflanker of positions, and in this role it was a terrifying sight. Ludendorff himself, in a report written on 11th August, said that the staff officers he had sent from Supreme Headquarters to investigate the defeat suffered by von der Marwitz's Second Army had told him that 'the troops were surprised by the massed attack of tanks, and lost their heads when the tanks suddenly appeared behind them, having broken through under cover of natural and artificial fog . . .'

Moreover, the German technique after losing ground had always been to regain it by instant counterattack. It was a highly-effective technique, and it had kept the battle lines intact over the best part of four years. Yet now, under the impact of the new form of war, it began to be abandoned. Exactly a week after 8th August the German

A German A7V tank attacks through a French village

General Sir Henry Wilson, Chief of the Imperial General Staff, inspects French troops

21st Infantry Division issued an order which reluctantly acknowledged that 'counterattacks against enemy infantry supported by tanks do not offer any chance of success. They must, therefore, be launched only if the tanks have been put out of action...'

Technological inferiority is infinitely depressing to a soldier. Fuller, the chief tank propagandist of 1918, held the view that 'weapons form 99 per cent of victory . . .' One wonders how far his view would have been modified by the war in Vietnam half a century later. In the circumstances of 1918, however, he was right. The tank *had*

happened before. Victory or defeat on the Western Front were expressed in terms of minor tactics. Morale was built around them. The momentary loss of nerve in the German Second Army was matched by a loss of nerve very much farther up the command structure – and by a gradually seeping realisation that the German army, for all its valour, sacrifice and discipline, had been overtaken in the technology of war. That was decisive.

Looking back in the comfort of hindsight, of course, we can see that German soldiers, in the short term at least, were too pessimistic. We know that after a few days of battle, the whole of the British Tank Corps would have to be withdrawn for rest, replacement, or repair, and that tanks could not continue to be used on the scale of 8th August. Yet even had the war continued into 1919, the tank would eventually have prevailed. In the Allied command, the tank idea had finally broken through, and the German army fighting the hypothetical campaigns of 1919 would have faced armoured attack on a scale which dwarfed that of the Battle of Amiens. Even before the battle, the British Chief of the Imperial General Staff, Sir Henry Wilson, had on 25th July sent Haig a memorandum concerning policy for the following year. It fixed a date for a decisive stroke: 'not later than July 1, 1919 . . .' It proposed sharp reductions in the cavalry establishment, and the mechanisation of some cavalry regiments into tank units. Most important of all, it put forward a general proposal for a gigantic armoured battle. It stated:

'The scheme put forward for General Foch's approval involves an Allied tank attack on a 50-mile front by a force of 70 divisions and eight cavalry divisions, supported by some 10,500 tanks. Of this striking force, it is proposed that the British contingent should be 20 divisions, with about 3,000 tanks, in addition to about 7,300 mechanical tractors for the cross-country transport of ammunition and

revolutionised minor tactics, and there had never been a war in which minor tactics were so inextricably mingled with major strategy. What happened over a mile or two of front around Amiens would have a profound effect upon major strategy, not because of its actual military consequences, which were probably inconsiderable, but because it had never

French troops rest on an overturned
German A7V

rations. The organisation, equipment and training of these 20 divisions, which amount to about half of the total British force in France, should have priority over all other requirements. The total British tank personnel required will be 35,000 . . .'

This remarkable plan did not impress Haig in the summer of 1918. His own anxieties about the battles he was actually engaged in fighting were certainly sufficient to occupy his mind. He wrote angrily across the cover of Wilson's memorandum: 'Words, words, words, lots of words and little else. Theoretical rubbish. Whoever drafted this stuff could never win any campaign . . .'

While Wilson's essay was certainly over-imaginative in some respects, Haig's judgment was too harsh. When Foch received the plan, he was very much more encouraging. He wrote: 'I agree in every way with the main principles of the study you have kindly sent me . . . Tanks are indispensable for clearing the way, and supporting the rapid advance of the infantry. They must be used in as large numbers as possible; consequently, construction must be hastened . . .'

Wilson's memorandum must also be taken the more seriously because it owed a good deal to a plan put forward by Fuller in May 1918, in his capacity as chief staff officer of the Tank Corps. This plan – it later became known as 'Plan 1919' – clearly revealed how, in the minds of intelligent and imaginative Allied soldiers, the tank was being steadily transformed from the limited wire-crusher and machine gun harrier of 1916 to 1918 into something much nearer to being a decisive weapon. The object which Fuller laid down in his plan was 'to strike at the brain of the enemy by attacking his headquarters and communications, and so paralyse his action.'

Fuller's theme was simple. He believed that the only true objective in war was the mind and will of the enemy commander. When these were numbed and ruined, he reasoned, the

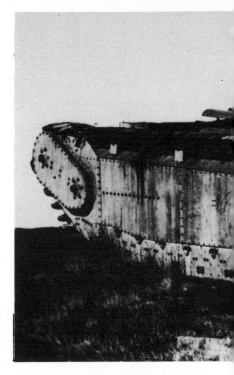

main body of the enemy forces would become helpless, like limbs threshing spasmodically without a directing brain. The idea had come to him during the Allied *débâcle* in March. He wrote later:

'What then did I see? Tens of thousands of our men being pulled back by their panic-striken headquarters. I saw Army Headquarters retiring, then Corps, next Divisional, and lastly Brigade. I saw the intimate connection between will and action, and that action without will loses all co-ordination: that without an active and directing brain, an army is reduced to a mob. Then I realised that if this idea could be rationalised . . . a new tactics could be evolved.'

Fuller's 'Plan 1919' attempted to evolve these very tactics. It envisaged a disruptive attack on enemy headquarters even before the main assault was launched. This disruption would be accomplished by nearly 800 tanks of a new fast type, which would tear through a ninety-mile front and reach

the opposing headquarters in about two hours, destroying the intervening divisional and corps headquarters on the way. Then a breaking force of nearly 3,000 heavy tanks would exploit the resulting chaos, supporting infantry and guns in seizing the enemy line. Finally, a pursuing force of 1,200 fast tanks would exploit and destroy in the role of armoured cavalry. It was a project which today may seem to have been ahead of its time, but to read Wilson's memorandum in detail is to be convinced that something like it would have been tried in 1919, if Fuller's main objective – the defeat of the mind of Ludendorff – had not been rather prematurely attained on 8th August.

One aspect of the plan which is often neglected today is that the machines necessary for its execution were already being successfully designed. The Medium A Whippet design was overtaken in December 1917 by Sir William Tritton's Medium C Hornet, which could deal with obstacles nearly

A look at the future: the Medium D tank

as well as the heavy Mark V, had a road speed of almost eight miles an hour, and a radius of action of 120 miles – compared with 45 miles for the Mark V and 80 for the Whippet. The end of the war came before the Hornet was in heavy production, and only thirty-six were built.

Meanwhile, a much more startling machine was on the stocks. This was the Medium D, which owed its origin to a Tank Corps headquarters conference of 28th April 1918. It was designed by Lieutenant-Colonel Philip Johnson, and it was the tank around which Fuller had built his plan for 1919. The Medium D was a revolutionary vehicle, able to cross wide trenches, but with a weight of under twenty tons and a road speed approaching 20mph. Its operating range was prodigious – about 200 miles. It was also amphibious, and successfully swam the River Stour a few months after the

The Mark VIII tank, a product of Anglo-American cooperation

Armistice of November 1918.

Not all projected development was in the field of the fast tank, however. A remarkable example of international partnership was now being given in the development of a new heavy tank, the Mark VIII, which was being carried forward by Britain and the United States. This machine was intended to be supreme in the break-in role assigned to the 'heavies' in the plans for 1919. It was 34 feet long and 10 feet high, weighing 37 tons. The armament was two Hotchkiss 6-pounder naval guns in left and right sponsons, and seven Browning machine guns (sometimes reduced to five in later models). The speed of the Mark VIII was between six and seven miles an hour, and it had an operating range of about fifty miles. The crew was twelve in the British-built tanks, and ten in those manufactured in America.

Under an agreement signed on 19th January 1918 it was proposed to build a factory in France which would eventually be capable of producing 1,200 Mark VIIIs a month. The tank components would be shipped to France from Britain and the United States. Thus engines, transmission, gears, and electrical equipment would come from America, while guns, armour, structural members and ammunition would be made in Britain. It was an advanced scheme of international cooperation for any era, and especially so for 1918. The production problems it faced were very considerable, and the estimated production figures were certainly over-optimistic. Yet there can be no doubt that the whole vast scheme presaged an enormous expansion of the entire Allied tank force – especially since the United States Army was already establishing the nucleus of a tank force, using two light battalions of French Renaults under a soldier with a name destined to become famous in the field of armoured war, Colonel George S Patton.

In the minds of the Allied command, indeed, the armoured breakthrough

was being made. Beside the thinking of men like Fuller, the ideas of Ludendorff in 1918 were mediaeval. Beside the Whippet, the Medium Mark D, the Mark V and the Mark VIII, German tank equipment – still confined to a handful of A7Vs – was ludicrously inadequate. All that German technology was offering in 1918 was a lozenge-shaped tank on British lines known as the A7VU, of which only one was built. Also under construction were two so-called K tanks, each weighing 165 tons, and armed with four 77mm guns. These two dinosaur-like monsters were expected to heave themselves across the trench system

of the Western Front. However, the war ended before they were completed. They would have been a ridiculously small counterweight to the armoured onslaught of Wilson's memorandum, or to Fuller's 'Plan 1919.'

From the point of view of the advancement of military theory, the Armistice of November 1918 came too soon. Not unnaturally, the instinct after the war was to dismantle the whole vast array of equipment and projects being prepared for campaigns which would not take place. In Britain and America, the tank idea was an early sufferer from this attitude. It is arguable that if some approximation

Lieutenant-Colonel George S Patton with a Renault FT in July 1918. He was in command of the nucleus of an American tank force at this time

to Fuller's Plan 1919 had actually been fought on the ground in that year the potentialities of the *blitzkrieg* would have received acknowledgment in the military establishments of Britain and France twenty years before they finally did. The armoured breakthrough of 1918 was soon distorted, minimised, almost forgotten. The next armoured breakthrough would not come until 1940, and then it would change the history of the world.

157

The Mark VIII, designed for the break-in role

Bibliography

Amiens 1918 by Gregory Blaxland (Muller, London. International Publication Service, New York)

Australian Victories in France 1918 by J Monash (Hutchinson, London)

Memoirs of an Unconventional Soldier by J F C Fuller (Nicholson and Watson, Redhill)

Military Operations: France and Belgium 1918, Volume V (HMSO, London)

My War Memoirs by Erich Ludendorff (Hutchinson, London)

1918: The Last Act by Barrie Pitt (Cassell, London. Ballantine, New York)

Tanks in the Great War by J F C Fuller (Murray, London)

The AIF in France 1918: Volume V of the Official History of Australia in the War (Angus and Robertson, London)

The Private Papers of Douglas Haig 1914-1919 edited by Robert Blake (Eyre and Spottiswoode, London. Verry, Mystic, Conn)

The Story of the Fourth Army by A Montgomery (Hodder and Stoughton, London)

The Tank by Douglas Orgill (Heinemann, London)